NORFOLK

NORTH SEA

The County returns 4 Members.

HOLKHAM HALL

NORWICH CATHEDRAL

LINCOLN SHIRE

CAMBRIDGE SHIRE

SUFFOLK

ANGLIAN *Images*

Haymaking

ANGLIAN *Images*

──RICHARD TAMES──

ALAN SUTTON

For Rachel Hicks and Joan Utting

First published in the United Kingdom in 1991 by
Alan Sutton Publishing · Phoenix Mill · Far Thrupp · Stroud · Gloucestershire

First published in the United States of America in 1992 by
Alan Sutton Publishing Inc. · Wolfeboro Falls · NH 03896–0848

British Library Cataloguing in Publication Data

Tames, Richard *1946–*
Anglian images.
1. England
I. Title
942.6

ISBN 0–86299–746–1

Library of Congress Cataloguing in Publication Data applied for

Endpapers: County Maps of Old England by Thomas Moule originally
published in 1830

Front Cover Photograph: Cavendish, Suffolk (*Barry Beattie*)

Back Cover Photograph: Thurne, Norfolk (*Paul Felix*)

Typeset Bembo 11/13
Typesetting and origination
by Alan Sutton Publishing Limited
Colour and duotones
by Yeo Valley Graphics
Printed in Malaysia

Introduction

The paradox of East Anglia is that it has for two thousand years played a decisive role in the life of the nation, yet somehow still contrives to give the impression of being a quiet backwater, left behind by the times.

Colchester is our oldest continuously inhabited city and the first place the Romans made their capital. Even after they founded London it remained the cult centre for the worship of the Emperor Claudius. The present castle, which stands over the remains of his temple, was built by the Normans to be larger than the Tower of London itself. In Saxon times North Elmham, now a village, boasted a cathedral. Suffolk still has some five hundred villages which can trace their origins back, not to Domesday, but to before the Vikings came, over two centuries earlier. Thetford was in early medieval times England's fourth largest city. And in the last twenty years the region's population has grown faster than any other in Britain.

Yet, as recently as 1903 a contributor to the *Essex Review* could write:

To all except hunting men, the large district of Essex now known as 'the Roothings' but formerly as 'the Rodings' is a veritable terra incognita. *The eight (formerly nine) small parishes composing the district take their common name from the river Roding which flows through their midst. . . . All are thinly populated and purely rural. Their combined population amounted at the last census to 1885 souls, an average of 102 persons to the square mile, against an average of 704 to the square mile for the whole county. The Roothings lie on the way to nowhere in particular. They are neither intersected nor approached by any important main road; they contain no ancient earthwork, no picturesque ruin, no large church, not even a single monumental brass, and no residence of greater consequence than a large farmhouse or country parsonage. No district so near London (and the nearest portion of the Roothings lies within twenty-five miles of St Paul's) is so little known.*

Considering its proximity to London, Essex entered the twentieth century as a curiously old-fashioned county, apparently bypassed by industrialization and seemingly resistant even, except along the margin of the Thames, to the relentless suburbanization which was transforming the rest of the Home Counties. At least that was how it was seen by the novelist H.G. Wells, a newcomer to the county. In *Mr Britling Sees it Through* Wells has Mr Britling instruct an American visitor on the vital differences between stick-in-the-mud Essex and go-ahead Surrey:

. . . lots of this country here has five- or six-hundred-year-old families still flourishing. That's why Essex is so much more genuinely Old England than Surrey . . . And then there are oaks and hornbeams in the park about Claverings that have echoed to the howling of wolves and the clank of men in armour. All the old farms here are moated – because of the wolves. . . .

Surrey is full of rich stockbrokers, company-promoters, bookies, judges, newspaper-proprietors. . . . They do something to the old places – I don't know what they do – but instantly the countryside becomes a villadom. . . . This Essex and yonder

Smacks, Lowestoft

Surrey are as different as Russia and Germany. . . . Those Surrey people are not properly English at all. They are strenuous. You have to get on or get out. . . . They dress for dinner. They dress for everything. . . .

Now here in Essex we're as lax as the eighteenth century. We hunt in any old clothes. . . . Our roses and oaks are wonderful; that alone shows that this is the real England. If I wanted to play golf – which I don't, being a decent Essex man – I should have to motor ten miles into Hertfordshire. And for rheumatics and longevity Surrey can't touch us. This country is a part of the real England – England outside London and outside manufactures. It is one with Wessex and Mercia or old Yorkshire. . . . And it's the essential England still. . . .

Twenty years ago, in an essay entitled 'The Essential East Anglia', James Wentworth Day wrote, half-facetiously, half-pugnaciously, as was his wont:

For the purpose of this chapter I have been asked by the Editor (whom God preserve) to include the Fens and Essex as part of East Anglia. So be it. I do almost anything for money.

The present writer by contrast needs no persuasion that Essex is part of East Anglia. What unites it with Norfolk and Suffolk is not the land but the sea. The sea has brought them Vikings and Bretons and Huguenots and the Dutch. The sea has exposed them to the threat of invasion and the temptations of smuggling. The sea has linked the region with the trade of northern Europe and at the same time made it the backyard of the metropolis by providing cheap and easy transport for passengers and goods until the railways came along. Cambridgeshire, Ely, Huntingdon and their neighbours, which some consider 'Anglian' too, can lay no claim to have shared in these experiences and are therefore excluded from this volume. Theirs is a different story.

Flat and boring, slow and snoring? Not a bit of it. This

Pinmill on the River Orwell

Saffron Walden

is the region that gave birth to the poll-tax revolt of 1381, when the peasant rebels of Essex took a Suffolk man, Archbishop Simon of Sudbury, and hacked off his head on Tower Hill. This is the region which produced the foremost soldier of the late Middle Ages, Sir John Hawkwood, whose handsome tomb stands to this day in the cathedral at Florence. This is the region whose progressive agriculture fed the expansion of Elizabethan London and revolutionized farming two centuries later. This is the region which produced Elizabeth Fry, prison reformer, and Matthew Hopkins 'witch-finder general', which inspired the 'Norwich School' of water-colour painters and literary works as different as 'Twinkle, twinkle little star' and 'The Battle of Maldon', the last great Anglo-Saxon epic, composed a thousand years ago to mourn gallant Byrthnoth, killed by a poisoned Danish spear as his faithful followers fell to the last man in three days of slaughter.

A paradise for yachtsmen and bird-watchers, East Anglia also holds the nation's records for the lowest rainfall and the most hours of sunshine. Its man-made features include the Fens and the Broads, while Nature has given it the Breckland and taken the port of Dunwich back to the bosom of the sea. And what we lack in cathedrals we more than make up in churches, Norfolk alone having

more than eight hundred. Such names we have as well: Fingringhoe and Tolleshunt D'Arcy, Layer-de-la-Haye and Helions Bumpstead, Stansted Mountfichet and Wendens Ambo, Hatfield Peverel and Theydon Bois, Foxearth and Fobbing, Messing, Mucking and Ugley. And that's only in Essex. Norfolk chastens the unwary stranger with idiosyncratic pronunciations. Its coast alone provides Cromer (locally Croomer), Cley (Cly) and Happisburgh (Hazebru'), while inland there are East Dereham (Derrum), Wymondham (Windham) and Stiffkey (Stewkey).

In selecting from the wealth of material which might be used to convey a kaleidoscope of the region's past I have confined myself to the period between the Tudors and the outbreak of the Great War, when, for all its diversity, the region can be seen most readily as a unity. I have deliberately excluded such much-plundered sources as the Paston letters and Parson Woodforde's diary and omitted such eminences as Cardinal Wolsey and Admiral Nelson, whose fame was won far from their place of birth. That said, I can only hope that what I have included will content the region's resident as well as intriguing its visitors. If it gives even half as much pleasure to read as it has given me to compile I shall have been amply rewarded.

Gorleston Parade

Looking towards Beeston Bump

ANGLIAN *Images*

*T*he *founding father of English topography was John Leland, who took a precocious BA at Cambridge at the age of seventeen and was appointed by Henry VIII as Keeper of the Royal Libraries while still only in his mid-twenties. Exhilarated by the literary riches at his disposal, Leland conceived a grand scheme for a national survey, and told his royal master that he was 'totally enflammid with a love to see thoroughly all partes of this your opulent and ample reaulme'.*

For six years Leland travelled tirelessly, assiduously taking notes. Then, overwhelmed by his task, he went mad, dying a few years afterwards. His great labour was, however, not in vain because John Stow, the first great historian of London, made a careful copy of Leland's itinerary. This copy eventually found its way into the Bodleian Library at Oxford, providing a master-text for eventual publication in 1710. Long before then, however, it was to be used as a major source by William Camden, headmaster of Westminster School and author of Britannia *(1586), a scholarly survey of the nation's antiquities.*

The first great description of England to put its emphasis on the contemporary state of the nation was produced by William Harrison (1534–93), Rector of Radwinter in Essex. Unlike the tireless Leland, and indeed, Camden also, Harrison, who held the one living from 1558 until his death, was a stay-at-home scholar, as he cheerfully admitted to his patron, Lord Cobham:

I must needs confesse, that untill now of late, except it were from the parish where I dwell unto your Honour in Kent, or out of London where I was born into Oxford or Cambridge where I was brought up, I never travelled forty miles forthright and at one journey in all my life.

Harrison was, however, a judicious sampler of other men's knowledge and well-placed to gather it. Radwinter lies in the north-west of the county, just off the main road from Cambridge to Colchester and within twenty miles of the borders of Cambridgeshire, Hertfordshire and Suffolk. Harrison also had free run of the library of his friend, John Stow and thus, like Camden, also had access to Leland's notes, whose value he freely acknowledged:

One help, and none of the smallest that I obtained herein, was by such commentaries as Leland had collected of the state of Britain. Secondlie, I got some knowledge of things by letters and pamphlets from sundrie places and shires of England. The third aid did grow by conference with divers either at table, or secretly alone wherein I marked in what things the talkers did agree, and wherein they impugned each other.

Harrison's England is, therefore, seen very much through Anglian eyes and illustrated with examples drawn from his own immediate vicinity and acquaintance. Bold in his judgments, pithy in his expressions, Harrison, like generations of Englishmen, was uncertain only about which he disapproved of more – change or foreigners. English workmen he praised for being: 'plain without inward Italian or French craft or subtiltie'. Even English criminals were superior to those of effete

Europeans: 'our condemned persons doo go cheerfully to their deaths, for our nation is free, stout, hautie, prodigal of life and blood'. The Scots, by contrast, Harrison dismissed as: 'unapt to anie other purpose than to spend their times in large tabling and bellie cheere'. Foreign travel as a means of education aroused his suspicion as its supposed beneficiaries: 'bring home nothing but meere atheism, infidelitie, vicious conversation and ambitious and proud behaviour'. The prevalence of foreign fashions inspired him with particular disgust: 'except it were a dog in a doublet you shall not see anie so disguised as are my countrymen of England'.

Harrison's no-nonsense nationalism and common-sensical conservatism went deep but did not make him narrow-minded, for his *great 'Description', if suffused with pride in county and country, is also shot through with telling comparisons and a keen awareness of the impact on his life and times of events and discoveries which went far beyond Europe itself. That he also had a quirky sense of humour is evidenced by the painted rebus which long adorned a window in his rectory – a hare dozing against the background of a sunburst – 'Hare i' sun' (Harrison!).*

Harrison's sense that the nation was going soft is made clear in his observations on changes in housing which he saw as anything but improvements:

When our houses were builded of willow than we had oaken men; but now that our houses are come to be made of oak, our men are not only becoming willow, but a great many, through Persian delicacy crept in among us, altogether of straw.

Harrison was, however, objective enough to cross-check his own opinions with those of others:

There are old men dwelling in the village where I remain which have noted three things to be marvellously altered in England within their sound remembrance. . . . One is the multitude of chimneys lately erected. . . . The second is the great amendment of lodging; for, said they, our fathers, yea and we ourselves also, have lain full oft upon straw pallets . . . and a good round log under their heads instead of a bolster or pillow. . . . The third thing they tell of is the exchange of vessel, as of treen [*wooden*] platters into pewter and wooden spoons into silver or tin.

For a stick-in-the-mud Englishman, Harrison was well-informed about the differences between his own country and the styles of continental Europe and the ways in which these impressed foreign visitors:

The greatest part of our building in the cities and good towns of England consisteth only of timber, for as yet few of the houses of the commonalty (except here and there in the west-country towns) are made of stone. . . . Certes this rude kind of building made the Spaniards in Queen Mary's days to wonder, but chiefly when they saw what large diet was used in many of these so homely cottages. . . . 'These English have their houses made of sticks and dirt, but they fare commonly so well as the king.'

Harrison noted another contrast with Europe:

This also hath been common in England, contrary to the customs of all other nations, and yet to be seen . . . that many of our greatest houses have outwardly been very simple and plain to sight, which inwardly have been able to receive a duke with his whole train and lodge them at their ease. Hereby, moreover, is it come to pass that the fronts of our streets have not been so uniform and orderly builded as those of foreign cities, where (to say truth) the outer side of their mansions and dwellings have oft more cost bestowed upon them than all the rest of the house . . .

As a man who clearly loved his own fireside Harrison seems to have approved of the growing trend to make homes cosier and less draughty:

The walls of our houses . . . be either hanged with tapestry, arras work or painted cloths . . . or else they are ceiled with oak of our own or wainscot brought hither out of the east countries, whereby the rooms are not a little commended, made warm and much more close than otherwise they would be.

Harrison was forcibly aware that England's growing prosperity was not confined to well-padded parsons like himself:

Kentwell Hall, Long Melford

East Dereham

The furniture of our houses also exceedeth, and is grown in manner even to passing delicacy; and herein I do not speak of the nobility and gentry only, but likewise of the lowest sort in most places of our south country . . . many farmers . . . garnish their cupboards with plate, their joined beds with tapestry and silk hangings and their tables with carpets and fine napery, whereby the wealth of our country (God be praised therefore and give us grace to employ it well) doth infinitely appear. Neither do I speak this in reproach of any man, God is my judge, but to shew that I do rejoice rather to see how God hath blessed us with his good gifts: and whilst I behold how that, in a time wherein all things are grown to most excessive prices, and what commodity so ever is to be had is daily plucked from

East Dereham

Clacton-on-Sea

the commonalty by such as look into every trade, we do yet find the means to obtain and achieve such furniture as heretofore hath been unpossible.

Harrison on homes is eloquent, but on gardens he is positively passionate:

If you look into our gardens . . . how wonderfully is their beauty increased, not only with flowers . . . and variety of curious and costly workmanship, but also with rare and medicinable herbs sought up in the land within these forty years: so that, in comparison of this present, the ancient gardens were but dunghills. . . . How art also helpeth nature in the daily colouring, doubling and enlarging the proportion of our flowers, it is incredible to report: for so curious and cunning are our gardeners now in these days that they presume to do in manner what they list with nature, and moderate her course in things as if they were her superiors. It is a world also to see how many strange herbs, plants and annual fruits are daily brought unto us from the Indies, Americans, Taprobane [*Sri Lanka*], Canary Isles and all parts of the world: the which, albeit that in respect of the constitutions of our bodies they do not grow for us, because that God hath bestowed sufficient commodities upon every country for her own necessity, yet, for delectation sake unto the eye and their odoriferous savours unto the nose, they are to be cherished, and God to be glorified also in them, because they are His good gifts and created to do man help and service. There is not almost one nobleman, gentleman or merchant that hath not great store of these flowers, which now also do begin to wax so well acquainted with our soils that we may almost account of them as parcel of our own commodities. They have no less regard in like sort to cherish medicinable herbs fetched out of other regions nearer hand, insomuch that I have seen in some one garden to the number of three hundred or four hundred of them, if not more, of the half of whose

names within forty years past we had no manner knowledge. . . . And even as it fareth with our gardens, so doth it with our orchards, which were never furnished with so good fruit nor with such variety as at this present. For beside that we have most delicate apples, plums, pears, walnuts, filberts, etc. . . . planted within forty years past, in comparison of which most of the old trees are nothing worth, so have we no less store of strange fruit, as apricots, almonds, peaches, figs. . . . I have seen capers, oranges and lemons and heard of wild olives growing here, beside other strange trees brought from far, whose names I know not. So that England for these commodities was never better furnished, neither any nation under their clime more plentifully endued with these and other blessings from the most high God. . . .

Harrison's rhapsody proceeded from a proprietorial pride in his own horticultural efforts:

For mine own part, good reader, let me boast a little of my garden, which is but small and the whole area thereof little above three hundred foot of ground, and yet, such hath been my good luck in purchase of the variety of simples that, notwithstanding my small ability, there are very near three hundred of one sort and other contained therein, no one of them being common or usually to be had. If therefore my little plot, void of all cost in keeping, be so well furnished, what shall we think of . . . Hampton Court . . . ?

Harrison loved his garden. Thomas Tusser learned to love his farm, though little good it did him in the end.

Few today know the name of Thomas Tusser (c. 1524–80) yet he was once the most widely read of authors. He is even credited with coining such common sayings as 'better late than

Cathedral gardens, Chelmsford

never', 'look before you leap' and 'Christmas comes but once a year'. Many were to profit from reading what Tusser wrote but the author himself did not – despite the fact that his major work went through no less than nine editions or revisions in his own lifetime. Fuller gave a sketch of Tusser's life in his Worthies of England (1662), noting drily that: 'He spread his bread with all sorts of butter but none would stick thereon.'

In the preface to his Five hundreth Pointes of Good Husbandry united to as many of Good Huswifery (1573) Tusser informs the reader of his origins:

It came to pass that born I was
Of lineage good, of gentle blood,
In Essex layer, in village fair,
That Rivenall hight.

Which village lied by Banktree [*Braintree*] side;
There spend did I my infancy,
There then my name, in honest fame
Remained in sight.

Precocious musical talent won Tusser a position as a chorister in St Paul's Cathedral, from which he passed on to Eton and Cambridge before securing a position at court as a musician in the entourage of a nobleman for over a decade. Marriage induced Tusser to change the direction of his life, abandon court for country and take up farming at Cattiswade in Suffolk. A genuine innovator – or perhaps simply unrestrained by reason of his inexperience – Tusser introduced the growing of barley into the locality; but he does make it clear that he had to learn farming the hard way:

> By practice and ill speeding
> These lessons had their breeding
> And not by hearsay or reading.

From Suffolk Tusser moved on to West Dereham in Norfolk, then to Norwich, then back to his native Essex and finally to London where his fortunes went into terminal decline until he died in debtors' prison. He was buried at St Mildred's, Poultry under an epitaph of his own devising:

> Here Thomas Tusser, clad in earth, doth lie,
> Who sometimes made the Points of Husbandry:
> By him, then, learn thou may'st, here learn we must,
> When all is done, we sleep, and turn to dust:
> And yet through Christ to heaven we hope to go,
> Who reads his books shall find his faith was so.

One of the most controversial developments of the day was the enclosure of common lands with hedges and ditches. Contemporaries and historians alike have savaged this policy as a calculated attack on the co-operative spirit of the traditional rural community. Tusser, however, was in no doubt that enclosure was an essential precondition for efficient farm management, the alternative being to expose all to the bad practices of the worst:

> Example by Leicestershire,
> What soil can be better than that?
> For any thing heart can desire,
> And yet doth it want, ye see what.
> Mast, covert, close pasture, and wood,
> And other things needfull as good.
>
> All these doth enclosure bring,
> Experience teacheth no less:
> I speak not, to boast of the thing,
> But only a truth to express.
> Example, if doubt ye do make,
> By Suffolk and Essex go take.
>
> More plenty of mutton and beef,
> Corn, butter, and cheese of the best,
> More wealth any where, to be brief,
> More people, more handsome and prest,
> Where find ye? (go search any coast)
> Than there, where enclosure is most.
>
> More work for the labouring man,
> As well in the town as the field;
> Or thereof (devise if ye can)
> More profit, what countries do yield?
> More seldom, where see ye the poor,
> Go begging from door unto door?
>
> In Norfolk, behold the despair
> Of tillage, too much to be born,
> By drovers, from fair to fair,
> And others destroying the corn,
> By custom and covetous pates,
> By gaps and by opening of gates.

Poor Tusser, perhaps he should never have left London. His near-contemporary Kemp knew how to make even a temporary absence turn to advantage.

Norwich Cathedral

As a self-publicist few men of Shakespeare's day could vie with William Kemp, an actor who belonged to 'The Lord Chamberlain's Men', the company to which the playwright himself belonged. Kemp, whose genius for droll buffoonery made him the obvious choice for such roles as Bottom and Falstaff, was, though short and stout, also remarkably light on his feet and excelled at the jigs which often punctuated or concluded theatre performances. In 1599, unaided by the Bard, he set himself to undertake the most extraordinary performance of his life by morris-dancing all the way from London to Norwich. The following year his own account of his feat appeared as Kemps nine daies wonder (though in fact the journey took over three weeks).

The ostensible purpose of this purposeless odyssey was to convey the greetings of the Lord Mayor of London to his opposite number in Norwich. Kemp, therefore, set off from in front of the Lord Mayor's residence, in the company of William Bee, his servant, Tom Slye, who was to improvise accompaniment on the tabor (pipe) and drum, and George Sprat, who served as a sort of umpire to see that Kemp really did dance all the way.

Averaging some three miles an hour overall Kemp only got as far as Mile End, a mile beyond the Tower, on the first day, so great, he claimed, was the press of the crowd. A large following saw him over Bow Bridge which crossed the Lea, marking the boundary with Essex. At Stratford, just inside the border, he heard the roar of a baited bear, set on by dogs to amuse the patrons of a local hostelry. At Ilford, Kemp himself was set up as the amusement when he was offered a toast in the locally famous 'great spoon', which held a quart. Drawing no doubt on ample experience of the deleterious effects of liberal hospitality, Kemp diplomatically declined the offer: 'One whole drought being able at that time to have drawne my little wit drye I soberly gave my boon Companyons the slip.'

Following the line of the modern A12, Kemp passed on to Romford, where he was given a lift on horseback for the last quarter mile. The next day, watched by the eagle-eyed Sprat, he recommenced punctiliously at the point where he had stopped dancing. At Brentwood four thieves who had been preying on Kemp's well-wishers were seized. The actor himself recognized one as 'a noted Cut-purse, such a one as we tye to a poast on our stage for all people to wonder at, when at a play they are taken pilfering.' Between Brentwood and Chelmsford Kemp, who part-financed his caper by peddling haberdashery on the side, was gratified by the patronage of a prestigious customer: 'Sir Thomas Mildmay, standing at his Park pale, received gently a payre of garters of me; gloves, points and garters being my ordinary merchandize, that I put out to venter for performance of my merry voyage.'

By the time he reached the county town, however, the strain was beginning to tell:

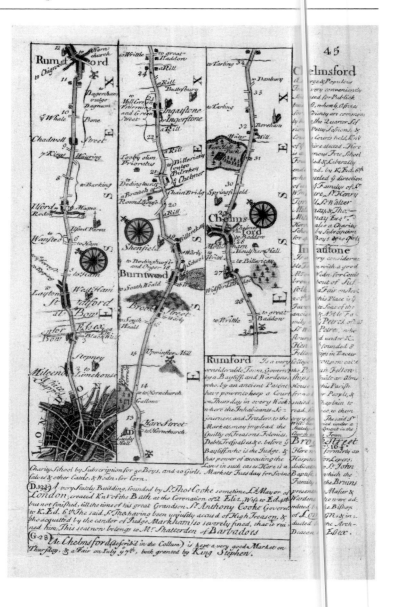

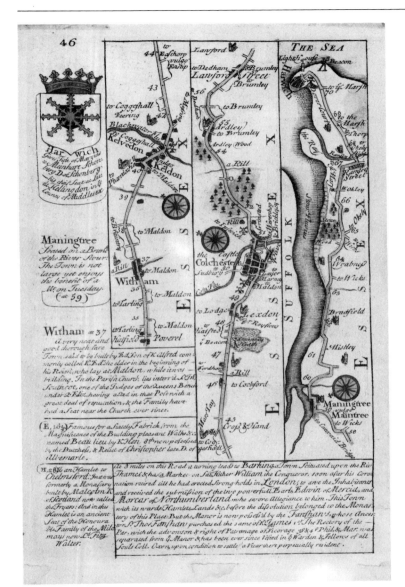

So much adoe I had to passe by the people at Chelmsford, that it was more than an hour ere I could recover my Inne gate, where I was faine to locke my selfe in my chamber, and pacifie them with words out of a window instead of deeds: to deal plainely, I was so weary that I could dance no more. The next morning I footed it three myle of my way toward Braintree: but returned back againe to Chelmsford, where I lay that Satterday and the next Sunday. The good cheere and kind welcome I had at Chelmsford was much more than I was willing to entertaine; for my onely desire was to refraine drinke and be temperate in my dyet. At Chelmsford a mayde not passing fourteene yeares of age . . . made request to her master and dame that she might daunce the Morrice with me in a great large roome. They being intreated, I was soone wonne to fit her with bels; besides, she would have the old fashion, with napking on her arms; and to our jumps we fell. A whole houre she held out; but then, being ready to lye down, I left her off; but thus much in her praise, I would have challenged the strongest man in Chelmsford, and amongst many I think few would have done so much.

The road from Chelmsford to Braintree was notoriously bad, with thick woods, ideal cover for robbers, on either side, and the way itself so muddy that Kemp was forced to long-jump one 'plash', landing up to his ankles in mud. A boy following him tried to do the same but fell in the middle and dragged over a friend who waded into extricate him – 'I could not chuse but laugh to see how like two frogges they laboured.'

At Sudbury, just inside the Suffolk border, Kemp was challenged again. A local butcher swore to keep pace with him for a mile but gave up half way, thus provoking a further challenge:

As he and I were parting a lusty Country lass being among the people called him a faint-hearted lout, saying 'If I had begun to daunce, I would have held out one myle though it cost me my lyfe.' . . . I looked upon her, saw mirth in

Kemps nine daies vvonder.

Performed in a daunce from

London to Norwich.

Containing the pleasure, paines and' kinde entertainment
of *William Kemp* betweene *London* and that Citty
in his late Motrice.

Wherein is fomewhat fet downe worth note; to reprooue
the fl.unders fpred of him: many things merry,
nothing hurtfull.

Written by himfelfe to fatisfie his friends.

LONDON
Printed by *E. A.* for *Nicholas Ling*, and are to be
folde at his fhop at the weft doore of Saint
Paules Church. 1600.

fat sides and footed it merrily to Melfoord, being a long myle. There parting with her, I gave her (besides her skinfull of drink) an English crowne to buy more drinke for, good wench, she was in a pitious heat.

Kemp at last reached Norwich on a Wednesday but postponed his public entry until the Saturday to enable the gentry to travel in from surrounding areas and a good local crowd to gather. When the hour came he was piped into the city, where a huge crowd pressed so close that he inadvertently trod on a girl's skirt:

Off fell her petticoat from her waste but as chance was, though her smock was coarse, it was cleane. Yet the poore wench was so ashamed (the rather for she could hardly recover her coat again from unruly boies) had she her cheeks all covered with scarlet.

Kemp finished his epic venture with a spectacular flying leap over the churchyard wall of St John Maddermarket and was duly rewarded with five pounds from the Lord Mayor and the satisfaction of seeing his travel-stained leggings nailed up in the Guildhall as a monument to posterity.

Kemp's epitaph in St Saviour's Church, Southwark likewise acknowledges his unique feat:

Welcome from Norwich, Kempe all joy to see
Thy safe return morriscoed lustily.
But, alasse, how soon's thy morrice done!
When Pipe and tabor, all thy friends be gone.
Then all thy triumphs, fraught with streams of mirth
Shall be caged up within a chest of earth;
Shall be? They are, th'ast danced thee out of breath
And now must make thy parting dance with death.

Norwich remembers its famous visit with a less sombre but entirely fitting memorial. The local Morris dancing group is known as Kemp's Men.

her eies, heard boldness in her words and beheld her ready to tuck up her russet petticoate. I fitted her with bels which she merrily taking, garnisht her thick, short legs and with a smooth brow bad the Tabrer begin. The Drum strucke, forward marcht my merry Maydemarian, who shook her

Fields of rape, mid-Suffolk

Robert Reyce's Breviary of Suffolk *(1618) offers a picture of a county rather different from those of later travellers such as Defoe or Cobbett. Reyce writes as a long-time resident rather than a visitor and aims to produce a systematic survey rather than a series of vivid impressions. Acutely conscious of the social as much as the physical landscape, he reveals his priorities and prejudices in his sub-title:*

. . . a plaine and familiar description of the Country, the fruits, the buildings, the people and inhabitants, the customs, the division political and ecclesiasticall, houses of Religion, with all their several valuations, the chiefest men of learning, as of Divines, privy Councellours, martiall men, and Navigators of former times, with several other things of memorable note, and observation within the County of Suffolk.

Reyce, a native of Preston near Lavenham, was the son of a JP and was able to bring to his task the perspective which comes from travel and contact with learned men, having been educated in Geneva and being a life-long friend of the antiquary Sir Symonds D'Ewes of Stowlangtoft.

To the modern reader Reyce appears obsessed with social status, reminding us that the feudal spirit lingered on well into the seventeenth century. The contrast with Defoe, writing a century later, is striking; Defoe's preoccupations are almost entirely bourgeois. Reyce, however, diligently lists hundreds of lords of the manor as they were in 1315, records the names of eminent lawyers and 'martiall men', notes in great detail significant monuments and heraldic devices in churches and sets out extensive genealogies of noble houses. Reyce was clearly fascinated, as he freely confesses in his preface, by:

. . . the alteration of names clean worne outt, the revolution of families now wholly extinguished, the traces of antiquity, the memorials of our honourable ancestors, with the monuments of their best deservings, exciting us

to imitation, and the notes of their frail blemishes, admonishing us to eschew them.

He takes this obsession with reputation and the past to be wholly proper and widely shared:

. . . every one naturally doth foster in himselfe a secret longing, and silent desire for his ever continuance in this beautiful frame [*i.e. the world*], which seing it cannot possibly bee . . . yett hath the witt of man found outt this meanes so much as lyeth in him to perpetuate the reverend memory of his honorable parents, ancestors and much beloved friends departed, by erecting unto them the lively counterfeiting resemblances, effigies, pyramids, epitaphs, and monuments, as doth plentifully appeare in our churches cloysters, and many such consecrated places.

Reyce's survey begins with a brief account of the county's name, 'clymate', dimensions and borders, then describes the ten principal rivers before analysing 'The commodities from the Scituation', that is to say the advantages and disadvantages of its location:

. . . if navigable rivers, diversities of commodious havens, for exportation and importation, neernesse unto the quickest and readiest marketts of best trade, and with as little pirrill and smal charge as any other shire may bee justly acknowledged the sole meanes of a profitable and commodious scituation, then shall this shire of all such as truely know it, justly deserve that true commendation.

The very attractions of the county, however, constitute its major disadvantage:

I must confesse as all other earthly benefitts are accompanied with some incommodities, for it is objected it lyeth open and is ready for forreigne invasion, there bee so many havens, harbours, creekes, and other places of ready discent, that the enemy is soon entered. . . .

Nor were the threats entirely external:

Whereas it is said, being so seated as this country is nere the hart of the Realme, peopled as it is in the fatt of the land, which is a sufficient cause for the encrease of the great wealth, if trouble sometimes of domesticall insurrections, or civill devisions, should betide, it cannott bee butt that it should bee sooner desired, quicklyer spoyled, rifled, and overcome than any other remoter place should bee.

Reyce turns next to those features of county life which appear to him to be particular sources of pride: starting with 'A learned Ministry', Protestants grounding the validity of their faith on a deep understanding of Scripture. With Cambridge, a hotbed of Puritan radicalism on the one side, and liberal Holland (currently playing host to the future 'Pilgrim Fathers') on the other, Suffolk could scarcely escape being in the forefront of religious ferment and progressive opinion:

. . . the Lord hath voutsafed many singular benefitts as proper to this country among which this is one nott the least, the great number of religious, grave reverend, and learned ministers of Gods holy word, which are planted in this shire, travelling in the Lords harvest, with sound doctrine and upright life, from whence the Bishop of this Diocesse hath often said that hee was verily perswaded that there was never a Bishop in this Realme, nay in Europe, having respect to the smal extent of his Diocesses, that had so grave, so learned and judicious a ministry as hee had, but especially in this County . . .

Immediately after the divines comes the cloth industry, a revealing order of priorities:

Another large benefitt wherwith this County is furnished is the excellent commoditie of clothing, which of long time hath here flourished, enriching the Country and bringing thereunto nott a little praise and commendation. Now as the numbers of this trade are many, so are there clothes distributed into severall kinds . . . vented [*sold*] by the marchant into all parts of the world. It is observed that these artificers doe sett many poore persons a-worke which other wise knew nott how to live, especially of the women kind, whereof whole villages and townes, doe live and maintaine themselves by spinning, that know nott else what to doe to gett their living, in this trade it is reckoned that hee which maketh ordinaryly 20 broad cloathes every weeke, cannot sett so few a-worke as 500 persons . . . what with breakers, dyers, wood setters, wingers, spinners, weavers, burlers, Sheermen and carriers, besides his owne large family, the number will soon bee accomplished . . .

Underlying pride in the size and wealth of the industry and its complex division of labour, there clearly lurks an anxious fear of unemployment and its social consequences.

Reyce then reverts to an environmental theme, praising the very 'Aire' ('the physitians from the universitie have prescribed unto their sick patients to live in this aire'), the 'evennes of the Country' ('devided with little hills easy for ascent . . . with a most beautifull prospect') and 'the soyle', before admitting that Suffolk was almost entirely deficient in minerals:

I could never learne or read that any mineral were found in this country, how great soever the desire of some hath bin to search the hidden entrails of the earth in her deepest bosome for gaine; yett I have heard that in ancient time there was a mine of Gold oare about Bankeon in Herismere hundred, butt the experience of this dayly so much contrarying the same, made mee to receive it butt as an unprobable heare say.

Lavenham

Reyce takes the matter philosophically: 'Thus hath nature supplying us otherwise with a more ample countervaile, justly denied us the benefitt of any minerals or mettals within this country.' Nature had also been niggardly in the matter of stone:

Neither is heere to bee found any quarries of stone for the use of building, our best stone is that smooth peple [*pebble*] which serveth us for paving of courts and streets, and is either gathered in the plowed feilds, or fetched from the brookes, and ryvers, . . . or else brought from the sea shores, where at every tide it is washed and driven up through the violence of the waves, and surges of the sea beating up the same.

Like Harrison in Essex, Reyce was an enthusiast for:

. . . the infinite change of delightfull flowers, which by the skill of the curious gardiner are in every place growing, or of the supernumerary variety of most wholesome and sweet smelling herbes, which the wild feilds and pleasant gardens most plentifully affords to the curious searching herbalist . . .

'Corne' as the county's leading crop is given special considera-tion and again the concern for social order underlies Reyce's criticism of 'the greedy covetous marchant' who 'furnishes the ports from forregne parts with graine . . . oftentimes by stealth' instead of selling it within the county or 'unto our bordering neighbours'.

Corn and cloth were permanent features of the Anglian scene and it is, therefore, especially interesting to note Reyce's careful description of a recent but short-lived boom in hop-growing. At first it proved so profitable that hops were planted in the best meadows and 'unprofitable marshes and moores' were brought into cultivation so that 'many in short time proved wealthy thereby, many leaving their wonted trade, betooke themselves onely to bee hoppe masters . . .'. The result was a rapid rise in

rents and wage-rates and an almost equally rapid slide into disaster:

. . . yett when the owner lookt to have all these richly recompensed with a plentifull crop, behold such was the influence of the heavens, and the unkindness of the Seasons these sundry yeares past, that in the best grounds hopps failed; the prizes [*prices*] fell and the markett abated, which when the owner perceived, reckning therewithall his great charge, with most uncertaine gaine gave up this new trade, by reason whereof this kind of commodity is now come to decay . . .

Reyce continues the note of cautionary gloom when considering the impact of increased economic activity on the local ecology and especially on its timber:

. . . nothing so plentifull as of late dayes, what with multiplicity of curious buildings, variety of costly ship-ping . . . with the endlesse wars of this latter age, and lastly with the continuall desire of Marchants . . . for gain,

Cavendish

River Brett

hath almost utterly consumed our timber, a decay long since espied, but thereafter will be more bewailed, unlesse there be some universall care some waies to repair so important a ruine, whereof there is no great likelyhood, since generally there is more respect to a present private benefitt how smal soever, than to the great advantage of the common wealth hereafter.

One of the great transformations of the region in the seventeenth century was the draining of the fen country which marked its north-western border and stretched away into Lincolnshire and Huntingdonshire. In retrospect it may appear a grand and visionary project but at the time it roused suspicion and bitter opposition. The fenland people had their own way of life, deriving a livelihood from fishing, trapping, wild-fowling and reed-cutting. To turn the region over to agriculture would make them refugees in their own land. The fact that the Crown was backing the scheme prompted fears that, should it prove profitable, the king might use an unaccustomed financial independence to rule without Parliament. The Dutch consultant brought in to supervize the venture, Cornelius Vermuyden, was compelled to face out a long campaign of sabotage by local opponents of his efforts.

The Powte's (Lamprey's) Complaynte vividly reveals the depth of local feeling and also shows a keen appreciation of the economic interdependence between different parts of the region:

Come, brethren of the water, and let us all assemble,
To treat upon this matter which makes us quake and
   tremble;
For we shall rue, if 't be true, that Fens be under
   taken,
And where we feed in Fen and Reed, they'll feed both
   beef and bacon.

They'll sow both beans and oats where never man yet
   thought it,
Where men did row in boats ere undertakers
   [*developers*] bought it:
But, Ceres, [*goddess of agriculture*], thou behold us
   now, let wild oats be their venture,
O let the frogs and miry bogs defile where they do
   enter.

Behold the great design which they do now
   determine,
Will make our bodies pine a prey to crow and
   vermin;
For they do mean all fens to drain, and waters
   overmaster;
All will be dry and we must die, 'cause Essex calves
   want pasture.

The feathered fowls have wings to fly to other
   nations;
But we have no such things to help our
   transportations;
We must give place – oh grievous case – to horned
   beasts and cattle,
Except that we can all agree to drive them out by
   battle.

Great Neptune – god of seas – this work must needs
   provoke thee;
They mean thee to disease, and with Fen water choke
   thee;
But with thy mace do thou deface and quit confound
   this matter;
And send thy sands to make dry lands where they
   shall want fresh water.

And eke we pray thee, Moon, that thou will be
   propitious,

To see that naught be done to prosper the malicious:
Though summer's heat hath wrought a feat, whereby
   themselves they flatter,
Yet be so good as send a flood, lest Essex calves want
   water.

*Appeals for supernatural malevolence proved useless in the
end, although the outbreak of the civil war brought work to a halt
for some years. Ironically it was war which also brought the
project to completion. In 1649, the year of Charles I's execution,
Vermuyden was allocated the free labour of a thousand Scots*

Lavender harvesting

Stokesby, Norfolk Broads

taken at Dunbar. Later they were joined, supremely ironically, by five hundred Dutchmen captured by Admiral Blake in his victory over Van Tromp.

The drainage of the 'Great Level' was declared complete in 1652. When the Lords Commissioners came to inspect the work Vermuyden was able to point to forty thousand acres:

sown with cole-seed, wheat and other winter grain, besides innumerable quantities of sheep, cattle, and other stock, where never had been any before. . . . I presume to say no more of the work lest I be accounted vainglorious, although I might truly affirm that the present or former age have done none like it for the general good of the nation.

It was as well that Vermuyden could take such pride in his accomplishment. He had sunk so much of his own capital into the enterprise that he died in penury.

Rich in churches, Norfolk is thereby rich in graves and therefore in epitaphs. Whether they attempt to summarize a life, epitomize a character or point a moral, they seldom fail to instruct and more than occasionally amuse. The following small selection range from Elizabethan times to the Regency.

At Little Plumstead can be seen a brass portrait of Sir Edward Warner, Lieutenant of the Tower of London under Good Queen Bess. Apparently the task of encapsulating his qualities in a few lines proved too much for the author of his inscription:

> His virtues rare would not be letten passe
> Ne yet so worthy state in silence synke,
> But who dare write his golden gifts in brasse,
> Or blot his fame with rude and silly inke?

An alabaster monument at Holme-Next-The-Sea dating from 1607 has, by contrast, no doubts of the accomplishment it commemorates:

Heere under lyeth Richard Stone and Clemens his
wife, who lyved in wedlocke joyfully together
64 yeares and three monthes; of them proceeded
7 sonnes and 6 daughters, and from those and thers
issued 72 children, which the sayd Richard and
Clemens to their greate comforte did behoulde.

*(This score of eighty-five living descendants, while respectable
enough, pales beside that of Margaret Honywood of Coggeshall
in Essex who at her death could number no less than 365.)*

*The desire to make an inscription concise but memorable leads
almost inevitably into the temptation of punning as at Hunstan-
ton where Sir Nicholas Strange memorialized his father, Sir
Hamon, thus:*

> In Heaven, at home O blessed change
> Who while I was on earth was Strange.

*Mundham was the chosen place of retirement of the adventur-
ous William Harborne who crowned a varied career by serving
successfully as England's first Ambassador to Turkey. A verse in
brass sounds a confident note regarding his ultimate destination:*

> Behold a dead man's house, who full of days
> Retired here from the world. Desert and praise
> Should sit upon his grave in virtuous strife,
> This to construct and that to write his life.
> Here spare your coat, he needs no tomb in death
> Who embassaged for Queen Elizabeth;
> His next will be when at the general dome
> God sends his soul to fetch his body home.

*At Hanworth the demise of another well-travelled character is
recorded, with a touch of irony:*

> Returned to the universal place, the earth, where all
> must rest till the sound of the trump, William Doughty,

innoculation against small pox. Keen self-reproach is evident in the admission that: 'her fond parents, deluded by a prevalent custom, suffered the rough hand of Art to wound the flourishing root of Nature and rob the little innocent of the gracious gift of life.'

A monument at Heacham, recording the death of nine people in a Sunday boating disaster in 1799 unhesitatingly interprets the incident as: 'a warning to rising and future generations against rashly engaging in similar undertakings'.

A gentler note is sounded at Framingham Earl, the last resting place of Edward Rigby, a celebrated surgeon, who served as Mayor of Norwich and was also a keen agriculturalist. On the table tomb under which he lies near the chancel are two lines reminiscent of Wren's epitaph, which bids the reader look at St Paul's itself as his monument:

A monument to Rigby do you seek?
On every side the whispering woodlands speak.

The persecution of witches was prevalent throughout Europe in the sixteenth and seventeenth centuries. England was spared the worst excesses; but, within England, East Anglia, and Essex in particular, stood out as an area peculiarly prone to throw up witchcraft accusations. The first Act of Parliament against witchcraft was passed in 1563 and the last execution for this 'crime' took place in 1685. Essex, with a population of some one hundred thousand, produced about four hundred cases, Sussex only seventeen. The outcome of about three-quarters of the Essex cases is known; slightly under half resulted in guilty verdicts and of those found guilty just over half were put to death, though thirty-six more died in gaol of fever, which was usually taken as proof of God's visitation on the unrighteous. Execution, it should, however, be noted, was unusual unless witchcraft accusations were linked with charges of heresy, poisoning or treason or turned up evidence of murder. Many accusations were summarily dismissed after the accused produced before a court evidence of good character in the form of friendly witnesses.

who after 11 years travel to the Barbadoes and other transmarine countries, safely arrived home, and, when he had seen with great joy all his friends, took his leave.

A harshly cautionary note is struck in the church at Buxton where a tablet with a cherub marks the mortal remains of four-year-old Mary Ann Kent who died in 1773 as a result of her

It was an Essex man, George Gifford, Vicar of All Saints, Maldon, who produced one of the 'standard texts' on the subject – A Discourse on the Subtill Practises of Devilles by Witches and Sorcerers. *Gifford was by no means a fanatic and admitted that: 'Many guiltless are upon men's oaths condemned to death, and much innocent blood is shed.' Nevertheless he firmly believed in the death sentence, even for misguided 'wise women': 'Although they never mind to kill or hurt any, but to do them good, as they imagine, yet if they deal with devils they ought to die for it.'*

Modern historians often attempt to explain the 'witch-craze' in terms of the impact of a new capitalist economy on a traditional social order which, faced with surging population growth and confused by inflation (a phenomenon understood even less then than now), attempted to grapple with what it took to be a relentlessly rising tide of beggary and crime. The dissolution of the monasteries in the 1530s had removed the single most powerful instrument for damping down social discontent and relieving hardship. Women, it is argued, and especially single old women, would traditionally have had a claim on the charity of their neighbours, but in the harsh climate of the age found themselves victimized just because *their condition was a reproach to others. In a period of unprecedented religious turmoil what more natural than that a community, ridden by fear and guilt, many of whose members themselves lived on the edge of survival, should exorcise its tensions by turning on the most vulnerable with accusations that deprived them of the most basic rights or sympathy by linking them with the devil? And, as East Anglia was so close to booming London and its economy was so powerfully influenced by the capital's demand for food, cloth and labour, it is perhaps scarcely surprising that it should be so pervasively affected.*

The persecution of witches was at its height in the last twenty years of Elizabeth's reign. Despite the accession of James I, a self-proclaimed expert on witches, a more sceptical mood prevailed thereafter. The Chelmsford sessions records for 1614 record that:

Alice Battie of Toppesfield, widow, not having God before her own eyes, but being a common enchantress and witch, seduced by an evil spirit . . . with malice aforethought exercised certain evil and devilish arts . . . upon Thomas Perrie of Toppesfield, by reason whereof the said Thomas languished from 17 Sept to 3 Oct on which day he died.

Alice was 'transmitted to the Assizes and there she was acquitted'.

The disorders of civil war a generation later, however, produced an hysterical atmosphere which gave rise to the most famous witch-hunt of all, the dark hour of triumph of the youthful, self-appointed 'Witch-Finder General', Matthew Hopkins of Manningtree. Hopkins, the son of a Suffolk clergyman, scoured the region for over a year, venturing as far west as Bedfordshire, to produce for trial before the Earl of Warwick in July 1645 no less than thirty-six accused persons. Of these, however, twenty-nine came from the Tendring area around Manningtree, Hopkins' home town, where he claimed to have uncovered a coven of:

some seven or eight of that horrible sect of witches . . . with diverse other adjacent witches of other towns, who every six weeks in the night (being always on the Friday night) had their meeting close to his house, and had their solemn sacrifices there offered to the Devil.

Hopkins failed to prove this particular claim, despite the cruel methods he used to intimidate the accused.

English law forbade torture as such but allowed suspects to be deprived of sleep, clothes, food and toilet facilities. Little wonder that they could be terrified into lurid confessions within days. Of the accused, half were hanged, thirteen imprisoned and the rest acquitted, though the men among the acquitted were branded on the hand. Arthur Wilson, the Earl of Warwick's steward, later recorded his own account of these proceedings:

Hedingham Castle

Aythorpe Roding

About this time in Essex, there being a great many arraigned, I was at Chelmsford at the trial and execution of eighteen women. But could see nothing in the evidence which did persuade me to think them other than poor, melancholy, envious, mischievous, ill-disposed, ill-dieted, atrabilious constitutions, whose fancies working by gross fumes and vapours, might make the imagination ready to take any impression, and they themselves by the strength of fancy, may think they bring such things to pass which many times, unhappily they wish for and rejoice in when done, out of the malevolent humour which is in them: which passes with them as if they really had acted it. And if there be an opinion in the people that such a body is a witch, their own fears resulting from such dreadful apprehensions, do make every shadow an apparition; and every rat or cat an imp or spirit, which make so many tales and stories in the world, which have no shadow of truth.

Hopkins never had another year like 1645 when he had sixty executed in Essex, nearly forty in Suffolk and others in Norfolk and Huntingdonshire. But he went on to earn prodigious fees, assisted by a team which included a midwife and a brain-damaged simpleton. Hopkins' ultimate fate is as obscure as his motives. Trained as a lawyer's clerk in Ipswich, he was certainly ambitious and may just have been out for money. Another theory suggests that he was in fact a counter-intelligence agent trying to smash a royalist spy-ring. And he may, of course, simply have been a sincere believer in his mission. A tantalizing hint occurs in the church register of Brandeston, Suffolk, which records the wretched demise of its aged vicar, John Lowe, one of Hopkins' few male victims:

After he had been vicar here about fifty years, he was executed in the time of the Long Rebellion at St Edmondsbury [*Bury St Edmunds*] with 60 more for being a wizard. Hopkins, his chief accuser (who died miserably) having kept the poor man waking miserably

Somerleyton Hall

A summer's afternoon on the river, Norfolk

till he was delirious, and then confessed such familiarity with the Devil as had such weight with the jury and his judges. The truth is that he was a contentious man and made his parishioners very uneasy and they were glad to take the opportunity of those wicked times and get him hanged rather than not get rid of him.

This sad admission might stand as an epitaph for the times and, given that malice is itself a sin, witchcraft might indeed be believed to be the work of the devil.

Seventeenth-century Essex may have been scarred by warfare and witch-hunts, but wooing still provided a lighter side to life, as the following proposal, as coolly confident as it is complimentary, bears witness:

Amongst all the works of God, I delight most in beholdinge (the sun excepted) an amiable countenance; and such is yours, or none in these parts of England. Your face is a mappe of beauties, your gentle breast a cabinett of vertues, and your whole selfe a cluster of all the choicest delicacies:

River Gipping, Ipswich

Gun Hill, Southwold

Southwold

known as the 'New Draperies'. But by the late seventeenth century the two countries were embattled rivals, struggling for control of an expanding global commerce. As befitted maritime powers they tested their resolve in confrontations at sea. One such contest was the battle of 'Sole Bay', fought off the coast of Suffolk in 1672 and witnessed from the clifftops by the people of Southwold and Dunwich, one of whom wrote a rhyming account of the encounter:

One day as I was sitting still
Upon the side of Dunwich hill,
And looking o'er the ocean,
By chance I saw De Ruyter's fleet
With Royal James's squadron meet;
In sooth it was a noble treat
To see that brave commotion.

I cannot stay to name the names
Of all the ships that fought with James,
Their number or their tonnage;
But this I say, the noble host
Right gallantly did take its post,
And covered all the hollow coast
From Walberswyke to Dunwich.

Well might you hear their guns, I guess,
From Sizewell Gap to Eastern Ness,
The show was rare and sightly;
They battled without let or stay
Until the evening of that day,
'Twas then the Dutchmen ran away,
The Duke had beat them tightly.

but, in plaine English, not your pleasinge aspect, nor well-featured person, nor admired excellencies, nor weighty portion, fastened my affection on you, but your love (of this I have beene long persuaded) to a man (myself, I mean) so undeserving it. As for myselfe, I am thought worthy of a good wife, though unworthy of you. These pretty toyes, called husbands, are such rare commodities in this age, that I can woo and winne wives by the dozen. I knowe not any gentlewoman in these parts, but would kisse a letter from my hands, read it with joye, and then laye it up next her hart as a treasure; but I will not trye their courtesies, except I find you discourteous. . . . Lay your hand upon your hart, and resolve to say Amen to my desires. If so, I shall accept your portion with the left hand and your lovely person with the right . . .

In the sixteenth century the English and the Dutch had stood together against the common threat of Catholic Spain. Thousands of Dutch refugees had made their home in the eastern counties of England, enriching the cloth industry with their skills in the making of 'Bays and Says', the light-weight, fine textiles

In fact it was rather more of an even contest than the poem suggests. The English had been accompanied by a French fleet which, when they were both surprised by the sudden appearance of the Dutch, followed secret orders and withdrew to leave the

Pulls' Ferry, Norwich

two Protestant nations to destroy each other – which they then proceeded to do. The Dutch did sail away in the end, leaving the Duke of York, the future James II, to claim a victory. But the English were too shattered to pursue the allegedly vanquished Dutch. They had sunk or taken three Dutch men-of-war and wounded De Ruyter but at the cost of six ships of their own and the loss of two thousand men.

Certainly the people of East Anglia felt anything but reassured; the following year the fisher-folk of Sheringham in Norfolk sent a querulously worded petition to the Lord Lieutenant of the county:

Our Town Joynes upon ye Maine sea, as we are afraid every night ye enemy should come ashore and fire our Towne when we be in our Beddes; for ye Houses stand very close together, and ye Houses thatched with straw, that in one houres time ye towne may be burnt, for we have nothing to Resist them But one Gunn with a broken carriage, and foure Musquettes which we bought at Our Owne cost and charges; which is a very small defence against an enemy; and likewise we have no pouder nor shot for ye said Gunn nor Musquetts, when wee stand in need; Wee therefore humbly beseech your Honour, yt you would be pleased to consider ye danger wee live in, and that your Honour would grant us foure or five Musquetts more and half a hundred pound of pouder, and half a hundred pound of Bullet; and wee should think wee were able to defend ye attempt of a Dutch privateer.

Sir Thomas Browne contrived to live a quiet life in a century of turmoil, yet achieved sufficient eminence to be knighted by his sovereign and excite eager anticipation in the worldly-wise John Evelyn at the prospect of a visit. Even the normally restrained Cambridge Guide to English Literature *runs to the brink of hyperbole in concisely assessing his career:*

He was interested in everything. . . . But his interests were subjected to the profound reflection of an intensely poetic mind, which found expression in the finest prose the English language had so far known.

Browne's statue stands today on the Haymarket in Norwich, but though he lived the greater part of his long life in that city, he was born in London. Educated at Winchester and Oxford, he also studied at three of the greatest medical schools of his day, Montpellier, Padua and Leyden, before settling near Halifax, where he wrote the first draft of his best-known work, Religio Medici. *Composed only for his 'private exercise and satisfaction', it combines reflections on personal belief and the wonders of the natural world, betraying a mind learned and sceptical yet humble in the face of universal mysteries. The manuscript was widely circulated before a pirate print edition prompted Browne to produce his own perfected version.*

Settling in Norwich in 1637, Browne continued to compose idiosyncratic works, while successfully practising medicine and raising a large family. Indeed, his personality is nowhere better revealed than in letters sent to his offspring, such as 'Honest Tom', packed off to France at the age of fourteen to acquire some, but not all, of the ways of the world:

. . . be courteous and civil to all, put on a decent boldness. . . . Hold firm to the Protestant religion and be diligent in going to church when you have any little knowledge of the language.

Good boy, doe not trouble thyself to send us anything, either wine or bacon. . . . You may stay your stomack with little pastys some times in cold mornings, for I doubt sea larks will be too dear a collation and drawe to too much wine down; be warie for Rochelle was a place of too much good fellowship and a very drinking town, as I observed when I was there.

Years later 'Honest Tom' is about to set out on his first voyage as

Lavenham

Sheringham

a naval officer in the service of his king. Browne's advice is fussy but fatherly:

Honest Tom, – God blesse thee, and protect thee, and mercifully lead you through the wayes of his providence. I am much grieved you have such a cold, hard and sharp introduction, wch addes newe feares unto mee for your health, whereof pray bee carefull. . . . I am sorry you went unprovided with bookes, without wch you cannot well spend time in those great shipps. . . . If you have a globe you may easily learne the starres as also by bookes. . . . If they have quadrants, crosse-staffes, and other instruments, learn the practicall use thereof. . . . Forget not French and Latin. No such defence against extreme cold as a woollen or flanell wascoat next the skinne.

Browne's eldest son, Edward, followed in his father's footsteps to become a doctor. Professionalism is therefore mixed with paternalism in their correspondence:

Dear Sonne. . . . Extraordinarie sickly seasons worrie physitians, and robb them of their quiet; have therefore a great care of your health, and order your affyres to the best preservation thereof, which may bee by temperance, and sobrietie, and a good competence of sleep. Take heed that tobacco gayne not to much upon you, for . . . the bewiching qualitie of it . . .

If the profits of the next year come not up to this, I would not have you discouraged; for the profits of no practise are equal or regular: and you have had some extraordinary patients this year, which, perhaps, some yeares will not afford. Now is your time to be frugall and lay up. I thought myself rich enough till my children grew up . . .

Evelyn's exuberant account of his visit to this remarkable man spills over into a panegyric for his adopted city:

Next morning I went to see Sir Tho. Browne (with whom I had some time corresponded by letter, tho' I had never seen him before). His whole house and garden being a paradise and cabinet of rarities, and that of the best collections, especially medails, books, plants and natural things. Amongst other curiosities, Sir Thomas had a collection of eggs of all the foule and birds he could procure, that country (especially the promontory of Norfolck) being frequented, as he said, by severall kinds, which seldom or never go farther into the land, as cranes, eagles, and a variety of water-foule. He led me to see all the remarkable places of this ancient citty, being one of the largest, and certainly, after London, one of the noblest of England, for its venerable cathe-drall, number of stately churches, cleannesse of the streetes, and buildings of flints, so exquisitely headed and squared, as I was much astonished at; but he told me they had lost the art of squaring the flints, in which they once so much excell'd, and of which the churches, best houses, and walls, are built. . . . The suburbs are large, the prospects sweete, with other amenities, not omitting the flower gardens, in which all the inhabitants excel . . .

Thomas Browne's near contemporary John Ray (1627–1705) has only very recently been honoured with a statue, which stands in Braintree, the nearest town to his natal village of Black Notley. When the proposal for a statue was first mooted the headline reaction of the local newspaper was – John Who? Since that time the rapid growth of a 'green' awareness among the general public has begun to rescue 'the father of English natural history' from obscurity. That great naturalist, Gilbert White, curate of Selborne in Hampshire, referred to him as: '. . . the excellent Mr Ray . . . the only describer that conveys some precise idea in every term or word.' Not only did Ray attempt a complete schematic classification of the plant and animal kingdoms, he was also the first scientist to use the word 'species' in its modern sense.

Unlike Thomas Browne, John Ray did not manage to survive the whirligig of political change unscathed, as the following letter to a friend makes clear:

I am now in Essex, where I intend to continue till Bartholomew Day be past. I am as good as resolved not to subscribe the declaration in the Act of Uniformity and soe can expect no other than the deprivation of my fellowship. I must stay hereabouts to make up my accounts, and to dispose of my goods, till about Michaelmas. Many of our ministers in this county will be deprived upon this act, and those the most able and considerable. I shall now cast myself upon Providence and good friends. Liberty is a sweet thing.

Ruins of Beeston Priory

Steeple Bumpstead

Ray was, indeed, deprived of his fellowship at Trinity College, Cambridge but had the consolation of being elected a Fellow of the newly-established Royal Society in 1667. In 1679 he retired to Black Notley where he spent the last twenty-five years of his life in the house he had built for his mother. Shortly after his move he confided to the biographer John Aubrey: 'To tell you the truth this country wherein I live is barren of wits; here being but few either of the gentry or clergy who mind anything that is ingenious.' Aubrey remained a regular correspondent, supplying him with such gems as the intelligence that: 'Sir Christopher Wren told me once [eating of strawberries] that if one that has a wound in the head eats them it is mortal.'

In a work published in 1691 as The Wisdom of God manifested in the Works of Creation *Ray reveals how his great accomplishment rested on painstaking local field-work:*

Having this Summer, Ann. 1691, with some diligence prosecuted the History of our English insects, and making collections of the several Species of each Tribe, but particularly and especially of the Butterflies, both nocturnal and diurnal, I find the number of such of these alone as breed in our neighbourhood (about Braintree and Noteley in Essex) to exceed the sum I last year assign'd to all England, having myself observ'd and describ'd about 200 kinds, great and small, many yet remaining, as I have good reason to believe, by me undiscover'd. This I have since the writing thereof found true in experience, having every year observ'd not a few new kinds. Nor do I think that, if I live twenty years longer, I should by my utmost Diligence and Industry in searching them out, come to an end of them.

A decade later Ray, conscious of his advancing years, reviewed his life's work:

30 June 1702.

It is true of late years I have diverted myself by searching out the various species of insects to be found hereabouts; but I have confined myself chiefly to two sorts, viz: Papilios [*butterflies*], diurnal and noctural, beetles, bees and spiders. Of the first of these I have found about 300 kinds, and there are still remaining many more undiscovered by me, and all within the compass of a few miles. How many then, may we reasonably conjecture are to be found in England, in Europe, in the East and West Indies, in the whole world! The beetles are a tribe near as numerous as these, and the flies of all sorts not fewer. I have now given over my inquisition by reason of my disability to prosecute, and my approaching end, which I pray God fit me for. . . . As for our English insects, I think I may, without vanity, say, that I have taken more pains about some tribes of them than any Englishman before me.

A lighter side of Ray's character comes out in a collection of English proverbs he published in 1670 and which he confessed gave offence 'to sober and pious persons, as savouring too much of obscenity':

Penny and penny laid up will be many,
Who will not keep a penny shall never have many.

Good riding at two Anchors men have told,
For if one break, 'tother may hold.

The higher the plum tree, the riper the plum,
The richer the cobbler, the blacker his thumb.

A man of words and not of deeds,
Is like a garden full of weeds.

Children pick up words as pigeons pease
And utter them again as God shall please

In Samuel Pepys and John Evelyn the seventeenth century produced two of the greatest diarists in the English language, though both their diaries were to remain unpublished until the nineteenth century. Hundreds more unpublished diaries survive from the seventeenth century, testimony perhaps to the desire to record and reflect on the disturbing events of the day or, more likely, by keeping, as it were, a spiritual set of accounts, to enable the author to monitor his daily struggle for salvation.

In 1656 John Beadle, minister of Barnston in Essex, published a whole book on the art of diary-keeping, entitled The Journey or Diary of a Thoughtful Christian *which contained the following rationale:*

We have our State Diurnals [*journals*] relating the National affaires. Tradesmen keep their shop books. Merchants their Accompt books. Lawyers have their books of presidents [*precedents*]. Physitians their Experiments. Some wary husbands have kept a Diary of dayly disbursements. Travellers a Journall of all they have seen, and hath befallen them in their way. A Christian that would be exact hath more need, and may reap much more good by such a Journall as this. We are all but Stewards, Factors here, and must give a strict account in that great day to the high Lord of all our wayes, and of all his wayes towards us.

One who followed this precept was Ralph Josselin, vicar of Earl's Colne in Essex from 1641 until his death in 1683. From 1644 to 1665 his diary has an entry for almost every day and thereafter at least one a week, revealing not only the trivial round of village life but also the author's well-informed awareness of national and even international affairs. (An entry for 1652 comments on events in Holland, Spain, France, Poland, Scandinavia, Germany, Italy and the Middle East.) One of the earliest entries gives a pleasing glimpse of Josselin's personality:

5 September 1644

Stung I was with a bee on my nose, I presently plucked

out ye sting, and layd on honey, so that my face swelled not; thus divine providence reaches to the lowest things. Lett not sin oh Lord that dreadful sting bee able to poyson mee.

The following year saw Josselin running more serious risks on active service with the Parliamentary army:

River Wensum, Norwich

Thurne, Norfolk

I was out with our regiment; wee marchd to Walden, mustered, I sung Psalmes, prayd and spake to our souldiers on ye Common at Walden and also at Halsted; God was good to us in accommodating us and preserving us . . . our souldiers resolute, some somewhat dissolute . . .

In June 1648 the war came to Earl's Colne itself:

On Monday morning the enemy came to Colne, were resisted by our towne men. No part of Essex gave them so much opposicon as wee did; they plundered us, and mee in particular, of all that was portable, except brasse, pewter and bedding; I made away to Coggeshall, and avoyded their scouts through providence; I praise God for this experiment; it is not so much to part with any thing as wee suppose, God can give us a contented heart in any condicon, and when our losses may serve to advance God's glory, wee ought to rejoyce in the spoiling of our goods; this day I borrowed money for to buy hose, and borrowed a band to wear, having none in my power. I was welcome unto and pittied by my Lady Honeywood.

Two months later he records the end of the great siege of Colchester:

Colchester yeilded; infinite numbers of people went thither; ye Councell of Warre adjudged 3 to be shott to death. Sir Charles Lucas, Sir George Lile who accordingly suffered and Sir Barnaby Gascoine an Italian who was spared.

Josselin was greatly disturbed by the emergence of religious extremists in his own parish and his diary refers repeatedly to his efforts against them:

3 July 1655

Preacht at Gaines Coln [*Colne Engaine*], the quakers nest . . . its is an evill that runs much in all places . . .

15 July

Those called Quakers, whose worke is to revile the ministry made a disturbance at Cogshall, and were sent to gaole; oh, many fear the Quakers to ruine Cromwell . . .

10 September 1656

Great noise of people called Quakers; divers have fits about us, and thereby come to be able to speake; the Lord Helpe us to stand fast . . .

9 April

Heard & true that Turners daughter was distract in this quaking business; sad are the fits at Coxall [*Coggeshall*] like the pow wowing among the Indies . . .

11 April

Heard this morning that James Parnel the father of the Quakers in these parts, having undertaken to fast 40 days and nights, was die [*day*] 10, in the morning found dead; he was by Jury found guilty of his own death, and buried in the Castle yard. . . . It's said in the contry that his partie went to Colchester to see his resurrection again . . .

November of that same year saw Josselin intervening to keep the peace in the family of his aristocratic patron:

Mrs Marg. Harlakenden having laid out £120 at London, about her wedding clothes, her father being exceedingly angry, I appeased him, so that though he chid her by letter for her vanitie, yett he paid the scores.

Coggeshall

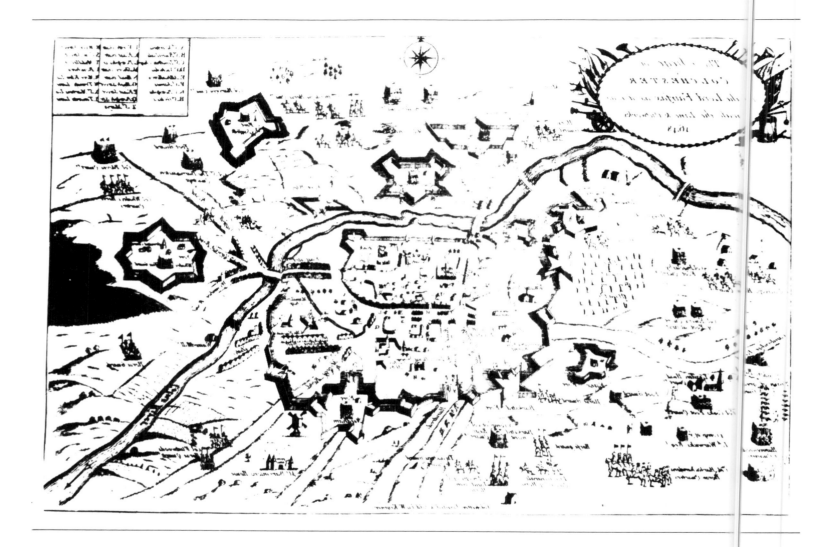

preserved from ye smal pox in our town and plague in the country, which is hott at Ipswich, Harwich an 100 dying in 3 weeks; at Colchester it spreads exceedingly . . . yet Colne, sinfull Colne, spared.

The diary of Joseph Buston, who lived in Coggeshall, the neighbouring village to Earl's Colne, paints a picture of a community which was, at the least, lively and at times positively riotous. Even his sister's burial involved the consumption of a barrel of beer, two gallons of sack and four of claret, as well as five pounds of sugar and the purchase of nine pairs of gloves (his father's funeral rated eighteen pairs). The actual coffin and burial accounted for little more than a tenth of the overall expenses.

Buston's diary chronicles the sometimes harsh measures used to maintain public order:

1680

A new Pillory was set up in Coxhall.

1681

There was a man, a stranger, whipt up Church Street, at ye cart's tail.

1682

There was a Ducking stoole set up in a Church pond. Ye widdowe Mootome paid £15.0.0 because she had a bastard; £10.0.0. of it was given to ye poore.

1686

The Poore that take Collection (i.e. licensed beggars) had badges given them to wear wch was a P & C cut out in blew cloth.

(In 1693 they were replaced with pewter ones marked 'Coggeshall Poor'.)

Indeed, the outraged father so far forgave his errant offspring that Josselin records the following month that: 'her father kept the wedding three dayes, with much bounty; it was an action mixed with pietie and mirth'. In 1658 Josselin recorded laconically: 'Cromwell died, people not much minding it.' But no one could be indifferent to the great event of 1665:

9 July

The plague feares the Londoners; they flie before it & and the country feares all trade with London. . . . the Lord stay his heavy hand.

20 August

Londons visitacon sad. . . . Colchester seeke into ye country for dwellings.

8 October

To thy goodnes wee own it with praises that we are

The accession of William and Mary was an occasion for general rejoicing:

14 February 1689

There was a day of Thanksgiving kept . . . for our great deliverance from Popery and Slavery by ye coming of ye Prince of Orange . . . and after Sermon ye effigies of a Pope was carried about ye Town and at night burnt in a Bonfire. And feb 21 King William and Mary were proclaimed. . . . The Coroner came and it was a Bayliff read ye Proclamation and a great many guns were shot off here that day and bonfires made at night.

The coronation two months later gave rise to further boisterousness: '. . . a garland was made, and oranges hung on it, and carried about ye towne, and a drum beat before it, and ye bells were rung . . . and a great many bonfires were made . . .'
If the cause of Church and King could evoke social solidarity, the outcome of a bad harvest could soon undermine it:

8 October 1695

The poor did rise at Coxall, in ye evening, to hinder ye carrying away of corne. And Johnathan Cable beat a drum to gather them together, for which he was carried before a Justice, but not sent to Jaile. The poor did rise at Colchester, and other places, about ye same time, and it was said burnt several waggons.

Sometimes the village found its enemies within its own ranks:

13 July 1699

The widow Comon was put into the river to see if she wold sink, because she was suspected to be a witch – and she did not sink, but swim. And she was tryed again July 19th and then she swam again, and did not sink.

An Essex butcher

Maze, Saffron Walden

River Blackwater

24 July

The widow Comon was tryed a third time by putting her into the river, and she swum and did not sink.

27 December

The widow Comon, that was counted a witch, was buried.

If diaries illuminate our understanding of families and communities in a particularly direct and dramatic manner, so, too, can the humble parish register. The parish registers of Halstead, Essex inform us of unusual deaths:

1617

Edward Clibberie, seniar (son of a former vicar) being excommunicated, was buried in the highway.

1620

A poore girlle that had no feete diing at the almushouse.

1656

Robarde Plumbe, he had bine bitten by a made dogs, was buried . . .

1658

Sarah Beadell who lived wickedly and died miserabelly.

1666

Thomas Clarket yt was stabbed.

1667

William Rand being shot to death by George Warrin.

The same registers also tell us of parishioners with nicknames such as 'Stammering Tom', 'Darling Baker', 'Blunt Smith', 'Ratt' and 'Stumpps'. These pale when set beside some of the real names that were recorded: 'Deaudaty Bragg. Repent Savage. Lanfrolet Chicken. Malchizedeck Hussick. Titus Vespasian Goodif. Golden Boosey. Pleasance Idle'.

What should a well-educated woman of quality know? Mistress Hannah Woolley, wife of the master of Newport School, near Saffron Walden in Essex, could have told you – though she might not have known when to stop. Mistress Woolley's publications included a Ladies' Directory, Cook's Guide, *and* Gentlewoman's Companion. *But her most popular work, reprinted at least four times between 1670 and 1684 was* The Queen-like Closet, or rich Cabinet; stored with all manner of rich receipts for preserving, candying and cookery. *Any idea that this was a mere cookery book should, however, be instantly dismissed. Consider, for example, the instructions for preparing that sovereign remedy, snail-water:*

Take a peck of snails (with the houses on their backs), have in readiness a good fire of charcoal well kindled, make a hole in the midst of the fire, and cast in your snails, and still renew your fire till the snails be well roasted, then rub them with a fair cloth till you have rubbed off all the green that will come off, then put them in a mortar and bruise them (shells and all), then take Clary, Celondine, Burrage, Scabeous, Bugloss, five-leaved grass; and if you feel yourself hot, woodsorrel; of every one of these a good handful, with five tops of Angelica; these herbs being all bruised in a mortar, put them in a sweet earthen pot, with five quarts of white wine, and two quarts of ale, let them steep all night, then put them into a limbeck [alembic]; let the herbs be in the bottom of the pot, and the snails upon the herbs, and upon the snails put a pint of earth worms slit, and clean washed in white wine; and then put upon

Lowestoft beach

them four ounces of cumin seeds or fennel seeds, which you please, well bruised, and five great bundles of Rosemary flowers well picked, two or three races of Turmerick thin sliced, Harts-horn and ivory, of each four ounces well steeped in a quart of white wine, till it be like a jelly, then put them all in order into the limbeck and draw it forth with care.

That recipe, which took at least two gallons of alcohol to prepare, was an everyday standby.

Serious complaints required the woodlice treatment. This apparently was variously applied to sore eyes, 'drowsiness of the brain' (her husband's sixty boarding pupils might figure here) plus scurvy and cancer of the breast.

Mistress Woolley was no less concerned with the serving of food than its preparation:

I have been invited to dinner, at which I have seen the good gentlewoman of the house sweat more in cutting up of a fowl, than the cook main in roasting it; and when she

upon wires or otherwise. All manner of toys for closets. Rocks made with shells or in sweets. Frames for looking-glasses, pictures or the like. Feathers of crewel for the corners of beds . . .

Sir Josiah Child of Wanstead, the great banker, was also an advocate of womanly accomplishments but his philosophy inclined more to the commercial than the practical. Noticing how much better educated Dutch women were than their English counterparts, especially in matters of business, he recommended a thorough grounding in mathematics. In the long run it would enable a woman to wind up her husband's affairs advantageously when she was widowed; in the short run it would incline her to calculation and therefore to thrift.

Most people remember Daniel Defoe as the author of Robinson Crusoe, *but this was only one of his more than five hundred publications, which ranged from ghost stories to political satires, from* A Journal of the Plague Year *to a history of the wars of King Charles XII of Sweden. By turns a soldier, merchant and secret agent, Defoe has been hailed as both 'the father of the English novel' and 'the founder of modern journalism'. And to his massive three volume* Tour Thro' the Whole Island of Great Britain *(1724–7) he brought both the novelist's imaginative sympathy and the journalist's eager interest in what is happening now. Defoe realized and revelled in the fact that the most important thing to record was not the country's illustrious past but its dynamic present. With change as his prime focus he could scarcely keep up with his subject matter, so he added to each volume an appendix covering:*

had soundly beliquor'd her joints, hath suckt her knuckles and to work with them again in the dish.

Gastronomy was, however, for Mistress Woolley a mere sideline:

The things I pretend greatest skill in are all works wrought with a needle, all transparent works, shell-work, moss-work, also cutting of prints, and adorning rooms, or cabinets, or stands with them. All kinds of beugle work

The improvements that increase, the new Buildings erected, the Old Buildings taken down, new Discoveries in Metals, Mines, Manufactures in a Nation. These Things open new scenes every day and make England especially shew a new and different face in many places.

Empire Day, Coggeshall

Defoe's foray into East Anglia began with Essex, a county he knew well, having run his own tile-making business near Tilbury Fort, which he characterized as 'the key of the river of Thames, and consequently the key of the city of London'.

The southern half of Essex revealed then, as it does now, the visible impact of London's overflowing wealth.

Passing Bow-bridge, where the county of Essex begins, the first observation I made was, that all the villages that may be called the neighbourhood of the city of London on this, as well as on the other sides thereof . . . are increased in buildings to a strange degree, within the compass of about twenty or thirty years past at the most. The village

Church End, Great Dunmow

St Osyth Priory

of Stratford, the first in this county from London, is not only increased, but, I believe, more than doubled in that time; every vacancy filled up with new homes . . . [and] . . . the increase of the value and rent of houses formerly standing, has, in that compass of years above-mentioned, advanced to a very great degree, and I may venture to say at least a fifth part . . . this increase is, generally speaking, of handsome large houses . . . being chiefly for the habitations of the richest citizens, such as either are able to keep two houses, one in the country and one in the city; or for such citizens as being rich, and having lived off trade, live altogether in these neighbouring villages, for the pleasure and health of the latter part of their days. The truth of this may at least appear, in that they tell me there are no less than two hundred coaches kept by the inhabitants within the circumference of these few villages . . .

Apart from the fact that the coaches are now luxury limousines and the 'handsome large houses' are twenty to thirty miles further east and north Defoe could well be describing the situation today.

Bourgeois to his finger-tips, Defoe (who had added 'De' to his birth-name of Foe) applauded this gentrification:

. . . this increase causes those villages to be much pleasanter and more sociable than formerly, for now people go to them, not for retirement into the country, but for good company . . . excellent conversation, and a great deal of it, and that without the mixture of assemblees, gaming houses and publick foundations of vice and debauchery . . .

Bourgeois disapproval is clearly evident in Defoe's attitude to the forays of the shooting fraternity to St Osyth Island, out along the coast, near Maldon:

In this inlet of the sea is Osey or Osyth Island, commonly called Oosy Island, so well known by our London men of pleasure, for the infinite number of wild-fowl . . . they go from London on purpose for the pleasure of shooting; and indeed come home very well loaden with game. But it must be remembered, too, that those gentlemen who are such lovers of the sport, and go so far for it, often return with an Essex ague on their backs, which they find a heavier load than the fowls they have shot.

As a professional writer Defoe was ever loath to omit a good yarn, even when he clearly had difficulty in believing it himself:

I have one remark more, before I leave this damp part of the world, and which I cannot omit on the women's account; namely, that I took notice of a strange decay of the sex here; insomuch, that all along this county it was very frequent to meet with men that had had from five or six, to fourteen or fifteen wives; nay, and some more. . . . The reason, as a merry fellow told me, who said he had had about a dozen and a half wives (tho' I found afterwards he fibb'd a little) was this; That they being bred in the marshes themselves, and season'd to the place did pretty well with it; but that they always went up into hilly country . . . for a wife: That when they took the young lasses out of the wholesome and fresh air, they were healthy, fresh and clear, and well; but when they came out of their native air into the marshes among the fogs and damps, there they presently changed their complexion, got an ague or two, and seldom held it above half a year, or a year at most; and then, said he, we go to the uplands again, and fetch another; so that marrying of wives was reckon'd a kind of good farm to them . . .

Of the northern part of the county Defoe noted

It is observable, that in this part of the county, there are several very considerable estates purchas'd, and now enjoy'd by citizens of London, merchants and trades-

Paddling

St John's Abbey gate, Colchester

Colchester

men. . . . I mention this to observe how the present encrease of wealth in the city of London, spreads itself into the country, and plants families and fortunes, who in another age will equal the families of the antient gentry, who perhaps were bought out.

Defoe's approbation is evident. It is lack of vigour in business that

dismays him, as when he notes of Colchester, three quarters of a century after the event, 'It still mourns, in the ruins of a civil war . . .'

Not that dynamic commerce was sufficient in itself to win Defoe's approval. Harwich, which he declared to be 'a town of hurry and business, not much of gaiety and pleasure; yet the inhabitants seem warm in their nests . . .' came in for sharp criticism for sharp practice:

Cattle market, Norwich

Ipswich

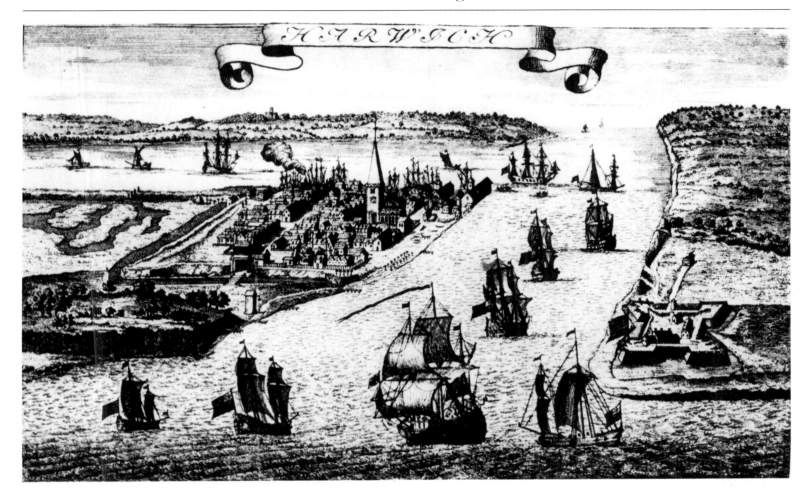

The inhabitants are far from fam'd for good usage to strangers, but on the contrary, are blamed for being extravagant in their reckonings in the publick houses, which has not a little encourag'd the setting up of sloops, which they now call passage-boats, to Holland, to go directly from the river of Thames . . .

Defoe was a fervent believer in the efficiency of the market,

despite the fact that he had himself been its victim as much as its beneficiary:

No man has tasted different fortunes more
And 13 times I have been rich and poor.

At Ipswich he was greatly impressed by the disastrous falling off of the great coastal trade in coal between Newcastle and

47229. SUDBURY: MARKET HILL, LOOKING WEST.

Market Hill, Sudbury

London, from which Ipswich shippers and shipbuilders had once derived fat profits. The cause he identified as cheap Dutch 'flyboats' taken as prizes and allowed by Parliament to introduce a fiercer note of competition. Defoe looked to the 'invisible hand' to remedy the situation:

I cannot think, but that Providence, which made nothing in vain, cannot have reserv'd so useful, so convenient a port to lie vacant in the world, but that the time will some time or other come (especially considering the improving temper of the present age) when some peculiar beneficial business may be found out to make the port of Ipswich as useful to the world, and the town as flourishing, as nature has made it proper and capable to be.

Defoe certainly found the locals 'very solid and entertaining in their society' and attributed this to 'their having a remnant of gentlemen and masters of ships among them, who have seen more of the world than the people of an inland town are likely to have seen'. Warming to his theme Defoe then extolls Ipswich with the calculated puffery of a modern property developer:

I take this town to be one of the most agreeable places in England, for families who have liv'd well, but may have suffered in our late calamities of stocks and bubbles [*a reference to the collapse of share values brought about by the speculative South Sea Trading Company in 1720*] to retreat to, where they may live within their own compass; and several things indeed recommend it to such;
1. Good houses, at very easie rents.
2. An airy, clean and well govern'd town.
3. Very agreeable and improving company . . .
4. A wonderful plenty of all manner of provisions . . .
5. Those provisions very cheap . . .
6. Easie passage to London, either by land or water, the coach going through to London in a day.

This last point is a typical Londoner's unconscious attitude to the provinces – how fast can you get back to the metropolis (i.e. reality)?

Defoe dismisses Sudbury as 'very populous and very poor' but Bury he salutes as 'a town fam'd for its pleasant situation and wholsome air, the Montpelier of Suffolk'. He declares that the county produces 'the best butter and perhaps the worst cheese in England', discourses at great length on the passage along the coast of 'our summer friends, the swallows', notes Suffolk's pioneering role in promoting the use of turnips for fattening stock and concludes his account with a stirring account of the annual poultry odyssey to the capital:

I can't omit . . . that this county of Suffolk is particularly famous for furnishing the city of London and all the counties round, with turkeys; and that 'tis thought, there are more turkeys bred in this county, and the part of Norfolk that adjoins to it, than in all the rest of England . . . tho' this may be reckon'd . . . but a trifling thing to take notice of in these remarks; yet . . . I shall observe, how London is in general supplied with all its provisions from the whole body of the nation, and how every part of the island is engaged in some degree or other of that supply; On this account I could not omit it. . . . They have within these few years found it practicable to make the geese travel on foot too, as well as the turkeys; and a prodigious number are brought up to London in droves from the farthest parts of Norfolk; even from the fenn-country . . . of whom 'tis very frequent now to meet droves, with a thousand, sometimes two thousand in a drove: They begin to drive them generally in August, by which time the harvest is almost over, and the geese may feed in the stubbles as they go. Thus they hold on to the end of October, when the roads begin to be too stiff and deep for their broad feet and short leggs to march in.

Defoe's account of Norfolk is one of almost unmixed enthusiasm:

... we see a face of diligence spread over the whole country ... throng'd with great and spacious market-towns, more and larger than any other part of England so far from London, except Devonshire and the West Riding of Yorkshire ... there is no single county in England, except as above, that can boast of three towns so populous, so rich, and so famous for trade and navigation, as in this county: By these three towns, I mean the city of Norwich, the towns of Yarmouth and Lynn ...

The county seat presented the visitor with a curious paradox:

If a stranger was only to ride thro' or view the city of Norwich for a day, he would have much more reason to think there was a town without inhabitants, than there really is to say so of Ipswich; but on the contrary, if he was to view the city, either on a Sabbath-day, or on any publick occasion, he would wonder where all the people could dwell, the multitude is so great. But the case is this; the inhabitants being all busie at their manufactures, dwell in their garrets at their looms ... almost all the works they are employed in, being done within doors

Defoe observes approvingly that:

The walls of this city are reckon'd three miles in circumference, taking in more ground than the city of London; but much of that ground lying open in pasture-fields and gardens; nor does it seem to be, like some antient places, a decayed declining town ...

It is Yarmouth, however, which enthralls him:

Yarmouth is an antient town, much older than Norwich ... better built; much more compleat; for number of inhabitants, not much inferior; and for wealth, trade and advantage of its situation, infinitely superior to Norwich

. . . the finest key [*quay*] in England, if not in Europe, not inferior even to that of Marseilles itself.

Defoe records in detail the extent and diversity of the trade passing through the port – herrings for the Friday fasts of Catholic Italy and Spain, woollens for the Dutch, timber and 'naval stores' from Norway and coal from Newcastle to London. The eulogy continues with praise for the honesty of the merchants, the skill of the mariners and the beauty of 'the most regular built town in England' which is even a moral paradise as well: 'It is also a very well govern'd town; and I have no where in England observed the Sabbath-Day so exactly kept, or the breach so continually punished as in this place, which I name to their honour.' Defoe admits, however, that there is a darker side to the picture, a price for this prosperity exacted by a cruel sea:

. . . this coast . . . is particularly famous for being one of the most dangerous and most fatal to the sailors in all England. . . . As I went by land from Yarmouth northward, along the shoar towards Cromer . . . and was not then fully master of the reason of these things, I was surpris'd to see . . . that the farmers and country people had scarce a barn, or a shed, or a stable; nay, not the pales [fences] of their yards, and gardens, not a hogstye, not a necessary-house, but what was built of old planks, beams, wales and timbers etc., the wrecks of ships, and ruins of mariners and merchants fortunes . . .

Defoe declares Cromer to be famous for nothing but lobsters (it is known for crabs today); 'Lyn', 'beautiful well built', derives its wealth from its situation, supplying 'six counties wholly and their counties in part, with their goods, especially wine and coals' and enjoying 'the greatest extent of inland navigation . . . of any port in England, London excepted'; of Ely Defoe remarks, as many have before and since, 'when the minster, so they call it, is describ'd, every thing remarkable is said that there is room to say . . .

Defoe's last stop, before passing into Cambridgeshire, was at Newmarket, which he treats with positively Puritan disapproval:

Being come to Newmarket in the month of October, I had the opportunity to see the horse-races; and a great con-

A Yarmouth 'Row'

Cromer

course of the nobility and gentry . . . but they were also intent, so eager, so busy upon the sharping part of the sport, their wagers and bets, that to me they seem'd just as so many horse-coursers in Smithfield, descending (the greatest of them) from their high dignity and quality, to picking one another's pockets, and biting one another as much as possible, and that with such eagerness, as that it might be said they acted without respect to faith, honour or good manners. . . . We enter Cambridgeshire out of Suffolk with all the advantage in the world . . .

The long, indented, often marshy coastline of East Anglia has for centuries provided an ideal environment for smugglers. That celebrated diarist Parson Woodforde of Norfolk unashamedly records purchases of wine and spirits which he knew to be contraband. Defoe refers sniffily to the matter as though almost too commonplace to be worthy of serious comment:

From Clye, we go to Masham and to Wells, all towns on the coast, in each whereof there is a very considerable trade cary'd on with Holland for corn. . . . I say nothing of the great trade driven here from Holland, back again to England, because I take it to be a trade carryed on with much less honesty than advantage . . .

A century later the Commissioners of Customs were offering £100 reward for the capture of a ruthless and vicious band operating in the same area:

A large party of men unknown were assembled within the port of Cley for the purpose of landing a quantity of Foreign Spirits from a Boat which was close to the beach. . . . George Monkman and John Nicholls, Boatmen in the Preventive Service, were patrolling the Coast, and detained in the said Boat, the two men they were endeavouring to secure, when the aforesaid party

beat them severely with bludgeons leaving Nicholls almost lifeless on the sand, and keeping Monkman a Prisoner, threatening they would kill him, till daybreak appearing, the said party disappeared.

In his novel Mehalah *(1880), which is set against the background of the Essex marshes, the Reverend S. Baring-Gould made it clear that smuggling was both a regular and widespread activity, an almost open conspiracy embracing whole communities:*

At the time of the Napoleonic wars, the mouth of the Blackwater was a great centre of the smuggling trade. It was easy for those who knew the creeks to elude the

Bury Road, Newmarket

Oulton Broad

revenue boats, and every farm and tavern was ready to give cellarage to run goods and harbour to smugglers. Deeds of violence were not rare and many a revenue officer who attempted to arrest and detain contraband goods fell victim to his zeal. On Sunken Island off Mersea the story went, that a whole boat's crew were found with their throats cut; they were transported thence to the churchyard, there buried and their boat turned keel upwards over them.

The villages of Virley and Salcot were the chief landing-places for smuggled goods, and there horses and donkeys were kept in large numbers for the conveyance of the spirits, wine, tobacco and silk to Tiptree Heath, which was the emporium of the trade.

The diary of Charles Hicks, a farmer of Great Holland near Clacton, shows that smugglers, too, ran risks:

1830

Richard Brett, a labourer belonging to Great Holland, was at work with others on the sea-wall. The day before Christmas they assisted some smugglers in getting a freight on shore. Having indulged too freely drinking gin, at night they were most of them drunk and could scarcely walk. Brett, in crossing the plank over the river from Lt. Holland Battery to Gt. Holland Marshes, fell into the river. His companions with difficulty got him out on the sea side, laid him by side of a hay stack near the Wall, covered him up and left him. The night was clear and a sharp frost; he was dead when they went to him the next morning. He left a widow and six children chargeable to the parish. A few years after, a fine young man of about twenty, named Martin Lott, of Lt. Holland, who had been assisting the smugglers, died from the effect of having taken too much raw spirit.

'To fear God, to help man and to hate all Tories' – such were the principles of 'Coke of Holkham', the foremost agriculturalist of his age and for over forty years a Knight of the Shire for Norfolk. When he entered the House of Commons in 1776 he was its youngest member, when he left it in 1832 he was the oldest. In 1837 he became Earl of Leicester, the first person to be ennobled by the young Queen Victoria.

Thomas William Coke had inherited the Holkham estate from a maternal great uncle who had already begun the work of its improvement; but so great were the changes that 'Billy Coke' made, raising its annual rental value from £2,000 to £20,000 in the course of his stewardship, that legend soon held that a visitor had been told 'all you will see will be a blade of grass and two rabbits fighting for it' and that the soil was so thin that it could be ploughed 'by two rabbits yoked to a pocket knife'.

Coke understood that the landlord and the farmer were partners, so he granted his tenants long leases to assure them that they would reap the benefits of their efforts and investments. He was also a great believer in sharing the benefits of practical experience, organizing what we would now call an annual convention at sheep-shearing time, where all-comers were entertained handsomely and invited to swap tips and opinions about crops, stock and farming methods.

'Coke's Clippings' were a county institution for forty years and on one occasion provoked a tribute as remarkable for its phrasing as its sincerity: 'Maister Coke and gentlemen, what I wish to say is, if more land lords would do as Maister Coke do, they 'ouldn't do as they do do.'

Visitors came not only to toast the master of Holkham Hall but to view the splendours of the great house itself, a palace which was essentially the creation of the Thomas Coke from whom 'Billy' had inherited it. The house seems to have quickly established itself as a 'must' for tourists, so much so that Letitia Beauchamp-Proctor found herself taking part in what was evidently a well-organized routine:

Holkham Hall

West Cliff, Cromer

When we came to the house the servant told us we could not see it for an hour at least as there was a party going round, and it was but just ten o'clock. We wished to have filled up the time with a review of the park and buildings, but there was no one disengaged to attend us. Therefore we were obliged to be shut up with . . . a whole tribe of people, till the housekeeper was ready. . . . Nothing could be more disagreeable than this situation. We all stared at one another, and not a creature opened their mouths. Some of the Masters amused themselves with trying to throw their hats upon the head of the bust, while the Misses scrutinized one another's dress. . . . At length the long wished-for time arrived. The good woman appeared, and we rushed on her like a swarm of bees. We went the usual round, all but the wing my lord and lady used to inhabit themselves: this was new doing up. I dragged them all into the attics, for which I believed none of them thanked me, especially one poor woman very big with child. I wanted to look at the sea, but it was so hazy, we could not distinguish it from a cloud. The tower library has been put in order; two librarians from London have been at work there ten weeks, and it is just finished. When we came down the party vanished. . . . I enquired, you may be sure, after her ladyship, and left all proper compliments. I thought I had missed none of the beauties inside or out of Holkham, but I found several I had not remarked before . . .

That was in 1772. But to Edward Rigby, visiting almost half a century later, it was not the house but the estate which moved him to rhapsody:

I have again been gratified in seeing one of the first places in the kingdom, whose scenery, combining the different picturesque beauties of rich, varied and highly decorated ground, of magnificent wood, expanded water, and extended prospect, including occasional views of the sea, cannot but delight every lover of nature, and more than meet the high raised expectations of the admiring stranger. But it has a character even surpassing the highest natural beauty; it has a moral character which leaves a more lasting and a more satisfactory impression, on the benevolent mind, than woods and waters, green fields, and the most highly decorated grounds. It exhibits man under his best features, and in his happiest state; it is the field of human industry, and it shews its rich reward; – talent and invention – science and experiment – the principles of mechanics – the discoveries of chemistry, and the investigations of natural history, are all here applied to the promotion of the first and most important of human arts . . .

In Gainsborough and Constable, born within a few miles of each other along the Essex–Suffolk border, East Anglia produced two of England's greatest painters. Both drew their inspiration from their immediate surroundings. Gainsborough, though famed today perhaps as a fashionable portraitist, far preferred landscape work. In 1788, the year of his death, he wrote to a friend, reflecting on the curious history of one of his earliest efforts:

Mr Boydell bought the large landscape you speak of for seventy-five guineas last week. . . . It is in some respects a little in the schoolboy stile – but I do not reflect on this without a secret gratification; for as an early instance how strong my inclination stood for Landskip, this picture was actually painted at Sudbury in the year 1748; it was begun before I left school; – and was the means of my Father's sending me to London.

It may be worth remark that though there is very little idea of composition in the picture, the touch and closeness to nature in the study of the parts and minutiae are equal to any of my latter productions. In this explanation I do not wish to seem vain or ridiculous, but do not look on the Landskip as one of my riper performances.

It is full forty years since it was first delivered by me to go in search of those who had taste to admire it! Within that time it has been in the hands of twenty picture dealers, and I once bought it myself during that interval for Nineteen Guineas. Is not that curious?

Constable was a boy of twelve when Gainsborough died. And whereas with Gainsborough landscape was perhaps a self-indulgence, with Constable it was a veritable obsession. Scorning Italy and continental scenes, he proclaimed that he 'was born to paint a happier land, my own dear England'. Why should any artist need to travel for inspiration when, according to Constable: 'No two days are alike, nor even two hours, neither was there ever two leaves of a tree alike since the creation of the world.'

But the uncompromising Constable still recognized in the polished Gainsborough the truth to nature which was his own supreme concern:

The landscape of Gainsborough is soothing, tender and affecting. The stillness of noon, the depths of twilight, and the dews and pearls of the morning, are all to be found on the canvases of this most benevolent and kind-hearted man. On looking at them, we find tears in our eyes, and know not what brings them . . . he delighted to paint, and . . . he painted with exquisite refinement, yet not a refinement beyond nature.

When it came to his own corner of 'dear England' Constable would admit to no imperfections, though he was aware that his attitude might seem a trifle subjective:

The beauty of the surrounding scenery, the gentle declivities, the luxuriant meadow flats sprinkled with flocks and herds, and well cultivated uplands, the woods and rivers, and the numerous scattered villages and churches, with farms and picturesque cottages, all impart to this particular spot an amenity and elegance hardly anywhere else to be found; and which has always caused it to be admired by all persons of taste, who have been lovers of Painting, and who can feel a pleasure in its pursuit when united with the contemplation of Nature.

Perhaps the Author in his over-weening affection for these scenes may estimate them too highly, and may have dwelt too exclusively upon them; but interwoven as they are with his thoughts, it would have been difficult to have avoided doing so; besides every recollection associated with the Vale of Dedham must always be dear to him. . .

(This self-justificatory sentence then carries on for another 183 words!)

Millions will know Constable's famous painting of Willie Lott's Cottage *at Flatford. Rather fewer perhaps will be aware that the famous* Haywain *was Willie Lott's farm wagon, going to the meadows across the River Stour by way of the 'Flat-ford'. Willie's 'cottage' was in fact an eight-room house with two attics. Willie himself was a semi-invalid who left his affairs in the capable hands of his brother John; but he still lived to be eighty-eight.*

In 1814 the Lott brothers subscribed £2 towards a village feast to mark Napoleon's departure for exile in Elba. This shows them to have been persons of some substance, though they were outdone, to the tune of £5, by 'Miss Tayler, A Lady that keeps a boarding school in the Street'. The following account of the festivities was written by the Rector, Dr Rhudde (£13 6s.6d.!)' John Lott copied it into his journal:

Be it remembered that on Saturday the 9th of July 1814, the Inhabitants of this Parish entertained the Poor of it, Men, Women and Children to the number of nearly 800 with a Dinner of Plum Pudding and Roast Beef with a Sufficient Quantity of Strong Beer at an expense of £113 13s.1d., which sum was raised by Principal Inhabitants in

Preparing asparagus

order that the Poor might Commemorate the Blessings of a General Peace, for which they had thanked God, by Religious Service on the Thursday preceding.

John Lotte annotated Dr Rhudde's preening official version with a line or two of acerbic footnotes: 'Mishaps, one of the Bells was out of repair and would not ring. And the Band did not arrive until after Dinner having lost their way and there was too much Bread and too little meat.'

The Lotts' fellow parishioners certainly had just cause for celebration. 'Boney' had threatened England for more than a decade and nowhere felt more exposed to danger than East Anglia, whose long, open coastline beckoned the invader. A decade before, the imminent threat of a French incursion threw Norwich into a frenzy of patriotism, as Charlotte Elizabeth Browne, daughter of the Rector of St Giles, well remembered:

Oh, what a spirit did it rouse among us! I could not then fully appreciate what now I remember with delight, the alacrity of our labouring classes in enrolling themselves, and forming local regiments of voluntary soldiers, officered by the very men against whom their enmity had lately blazed forth, and with most cheerful subordination obeying them. It was a lovely sight, even lovelier to me in retrospection than it was at the time, to behold England rushing to arms in defence of her own sacred home . . .
Military uniforms distinguished at least two-thirds of the male congregation and martial music accompanied the psalmody of the churches. . . . Thus we were in the midst of the excitement, and by no means idle spectators; for my brother, in whose character the soldier had reigned pre-dominant since babyhood, assembled all the little boys of the neighbourhood, addressed them in a patriotic speech, and brought them to the unanimous resolution of arming in defence of their country. Those whose finances extended

so far, bought real wooden guns and swords; others, impoverished by the allurements of an old dame who vended lollipops, were obliged to content themselves with such weapons as they could shape out of the hedge; a sixpenny drum and a twopenny fife completed the military equipment, while on me devolved the distinguished honour of tacking sundry pieces of silk to an old broomstick and presenting these colours to the corps, with an oration breathing such loyalty and devotion to the good cause of liberty and Old England, as wrought to the highest pitch the enthusiasm of the regiment, whose colonel was ten years old . . .

In the garrison town of Colchester the antics of a rather older group of boys in the nearby village of Coggeshall inspired the local theatrical company to offer a mocking farce:

Scene I. A Room. Mrs Dashit at a Glass, adjusting her Head Dress; Mr Dashit enters hastily.
Mr D. My dear, would you think it, I am a lieutenant, a lieutenant 'pon honour, a most respectable meeting, there was I myself, and twenty or thirty more gentlemen, all the heads of the town, six captains, the rest all lieutenants, three companies, hundred in a company, uniform superfine scarlet lined with blue, silver edging, gold epaulets, kerseymere waistcoats and pantaloons, bearskin helmets and ostrich feathers, swords and side knots; all is settled, all settled. Don't you think I shall cut a fine figure? But I can't stay for we are all going out to canvass for privates. Must come forward. . . . Everything is settled, quite settled; six captains, the rest lieutenants, three companies, a hundred in a company; no expense; devilish well managed, however; find their own clothes; so good bye dearee. Lord, lovee! what an elegant figure I shall make; scarlet, lined with blue, silver edging.

Colchester was, however, soon laughing on the other side of its

face. Ann Taylor (author of the immortal 'Twinke, twinkle little star') received the following alarming communication from her mother:

. . . On Friday last the principal inhabitants of Colchester waited on General Craig, the commander here, and received from him the most solemn and decisive warning of our danger, and of the absolute necessity of the female part of the population, with their children, and what effects they could convey, leaving the town with all speed. You will not be surprised to hear that we are all in the utmost distress and consternation. . . .

The Rounds are all going to Bath, Lawyer Daniel is packing up all his writings in sacks, and with his family, will send them to Halstead. . . . Shall we tarry or flee? . . . Do give us your advice by return of post. . . . Know, then, that this morning our dear Jane, Isaac, Jeff and Jemima, with a considerable portion of our property, set off in Filcham's waggon for Lavenham. . . . I was up last night to midnight, packing etc. . . . They are now, poor hearts, on the road, wedged in with chairs, tables, beds, soldiers' wives etc. etc. May the God of providence watch over them, and bring them safe to their journey's end.

If Defoe's masterly Tour *has any rival it must surely be William Cobbett's* Rural Rides, *the product of a series of tours undertaken between 1821 and 1832. Cobbett, a great John Bull of a man – 'just the weight of a four bushel sack of good wheat' – had been by turns a gardener at Kew, a soldier in Canada and a shopkeeper and pamphleteer in America, but he always thought of himself as a farmer. That elegant critic William Hazlitt observed of the prolific Cobbett 'his style stuns his readers' but admired his 'plain, broad, downright English' and saw his lack of formal education as a positive advantage 'he has no mortgage on his brain; his notions are free and unencumbered'. Cobbett's writings were, therefore, less remarkable for their consistency*

than for their vigour. When he enthuses about Suffolk he manages to do so in a way that makes even his compliments seem deftly back-handed:

I know of no town to be compared with Ipswich, except it be Nottingham. . . . The town itself is substantially built, well paved, everything good and solid, and no wretched dwellings to be seen on its outskirts. From the town itself you can see nothing; but you can, in no direction, go from it a quarter of a mile without finding views that a painter might crave, and the country round about it so well cultivated; the land in such a beautiful state, the farm-houses all white, and all so much alike; the barns, and everything about the homesteads so snug; the stocks of turnips so abundant everywhere; the sheep and cattle in such fine order; the wheat all drilled; the ploughman so expert; the furrows, if a quarter of a mile long, as straight as a line, and laid as truly as if with a level; in short, here is everything to delight the eye, and to make the people proud of their country; and this is the case throughout the whole of this county. I have always found Suffolk farmers great boasters of their superiority over others; and I must say that it is not without reason. . . . I remarked that I did not see in the whole county one single instance of paper or

The College, Framlingham

Flatford Mill

rags supplying the place of glass in any window, and did not see one miserable hovel in which a labourer resided. The county, however, is *flat*. . . .

It is curious, too, that though the people . . . are extremely neat in their houses, and though I found all their gardens dug up and prepared for cropping, you do not see about their cottages (and it is just the same in Norfolk) that *ornamental gardening*; the walks, and the flower borders, and the honeysuckles and roses trained over the doors or over arched sticks, that you see in Hampshire, Sussex and Kent. . . . In those counties, too, there is great taste with regard *to trees* of every description. . . . In Suffolk it appears to be just the contrary: here is the great dissight of all these three eastern counties. Almost every bank of every field is studded with *pollards*, that is to say, trees that have been *beheaded*, at from six to twelve feet from the ground, than which nothing in nature can be more ugly. . . . However, the great number of farm-houses in Suffolk, the neatness of those houses . . . and the admirable management of the whole, form a pretty good compensation for the want of beauties. . . . I did not observe a single poor miserable animal in the whole county.

To conclude an account of Suffolk and not to sing the praises of Bury St Edmunds would offend every creature of Suffolk birth; even at Ipswich, when I was praising *that place*, the very people of that town asked me if I did not think Bury St Edmund's the nicest town in the world. Meet them wherever you will, they have all the same boast; and indeed, as a town *in itself*, it is the neatest place that ever was seen. It is airy, it has several fine open places in it, and it has the remains of the famous abbey walls and the abbey gate entire; and it is so clean and so neat that nothing can equal it in that respect . . . but the country about it is *flat* . . .

Cobbett ends his encomium in a typically contrariwise manner:

That which we admire most is not always that which would be *our choice*. One might imagine that after all that I have said about this fine county, I should certainly prefer it as a place of residence. I should not, however: my choice has been always very much divided between the woods of Sussex and the downs of Wiltshire.

George Crabbe (1754–1832) is one of those poets who, famed in his own day, is now scarcely remembered or read outside the circle of specialists in English Literature. Eclipsed by the Romantics, he yet won the admiration of successors as different from one another as Byron and Tennyson.

Crabbe was born in Aldeburgh on the Suffolk coast. Educated at Stowmarket, he trained locally as a doctor but turned increasingly to poetry, religion and natural history. Abandoning a medical career, he sought literary fame in London where he endured hardship before attracting the interest of the eminent politician and man of letters, Edmund Burke. Burke not only saw Crabbe into print but also introduced him to the Bishop of

Storm, Aldeburgh

Wendens Ambo

Bildeston

Norwich, who ordained Crabbe and thus enabled him to gain a measure of economic security. This did not, however, make the poet a complacent recruit into the ranks of the comfortable. Although he could scarcely be classified as a revolutionary, Crabbe was keenly aware of the poverty and hardship of his native region. The Village (1783), his first major popular success, represented a frontal assault on the idealization of rural life which had been the stock-in-trade of so many English poets since Elizabethan times. Aldeburgh is therefore presented 'warts and all':

I grant indeed that fields and flocks have charms
For him that grazes or for him that farms;
But when amid such pleasing scenes I trace
The poor laborious Natives of the place,
And see the mid-day sun, with fervid ray,
On their bare heads and dewy temples play;
While some, with feebler heads and fainter hearts,
Deplore their fortune but sustain their parts;
Then shall I dare these real ills to hide
In tinsel trappings of poetic pride?

No; cast by Fortune on a frowning coast,
Which neither groves nor happy valleys boast;
Where other cares than those the Muse relates,
And other Shepherds dwell with other Mates;
By such examples taught, I paint the Cot,
As Truth will paint it, and as Bards will not:

Crabbe's next major enterprise was in a very different vein,
lighter but no less telling. The Newspaper (1785) lambasts the
Sunday prints in a manner which is still very apropos:

No changing season makes their number less,
Nor Sunday shines a sabbath on the press!
Then lo! the sainted MONITOR is born,
Whose pious face some sacred texts adorn:
As artful sinners cloak the secret sin,
To veil with seeming grace the guile within;
So Moral Essays on his front appear,
But all is carnal business in the rear;
The fresh-coin'd lie, the secret whispered last,
And all the gleanings of the six days past.

The Borough (1810) describes in twenty-four parts the life
and people of Aldeburgh. It is nowadays judged to be a very
uneven achievement, fame and success having rendered the poet
far less self-critical than in his youth. His description of the
poor-house, however, still shows the same keen sympathy for the
poor which characterized his earlier work:

That giant building, that high-bounding wall,
Those bare-worn walks, that lofty thund'ring hall!
That large loud clock, which tolls each dreaded hour,
Those gates and locks, and all those signs of power;
It is a prison, with a milder name,
Which few inhabit without dread or shame.
Be it agreed – the poor who hither come
Partake of plenty, seldom found at home;

That airy rooms and decent beds are meant
To give the poor by day, by night, content;
That none are frightened, once admitted here,
By the stern looks of lordly overseer;
Grant that the guardians of the place attend,
And ready ear to each petition lend; . . .

Alas! their sorrows in their bosoms dwell;
They've much to suffer, but have nought to tell;
They have no evil in the place to state,
And dare not say, it is the house they hate: . . .

Widows are here, who in their huts were left,
Of husbands, children, plenty, ease bereft;
Yet all that grief within the humble shed
Was soften'd, soften'd in the humble bed:
But here, in all its force, remains the grief,
And not one soft'ning object for relief.
Who can, when here, the social neighbour meet?
Who learn the story current in the street?
Who to the long-known intimate impart
Facts they have learned or feelings of the heart . . .

What, if no grievous fears their lives annoy,
Is it not worse no prospects to enjoy?

It is very appropriate that, although The Borough *itself is now*
rarely read, one of its most powerful tales, Peter Grimes, *should*
provide the story-line for the tragic opera created by Benjamin
Britten, Aldeburgh's most illustrious modern inhabitant.

George Crabbe the Younger in his biography (1834) of his
father, the poet of the same name, reminisces with evident delight
about his first visit to Suffolk relatives more than forty years
before. The warmth and humour of his description contrasts
strongly with the bleak picture of rural life which pervades his

The watersplash, Kersey

AT A MEETING OF THE
INHABITANTS
of
WOODBRIDGE,
HELD AT THE
TOWN HALL,
On the 14th. June, 1832,

For the purpose of deciding in what way to celebrate the passing of the
Reform Bill,
MR. THOMAS GRIMWOOD IN THE CHAIR.

Resolved unanimously,—That this Meeting feels anxious to celebrate the passing of the Reform Bill, in such a manner as may evince a high approval of the Measure, be of a public benefit, and at the same time not hurt the feelings of those who may differ in opinion. And that this Meeting conceives a Dinner given to the Poor, will be the best mode of celebrating so beneficial an event, and be far preferable to an Illumination, or other measure liable to abuse.

That a Dinner be accordingly given, and that a Committee be appointed to arrange all details.

That the Committee be open, and that any Inhabitant be at liberty to attend the Meetings of the Committee, and that five members be empowered to act.

That the thanks of this Meeting be given to the Magistrates for the use of the Hall, and to the Churchwardens for their kind and prompt compliance with the Requisitions of this Meeting.

That these Resolutions be printed.

THOMAS GRIMWOOD, Chairman.

The Chairman having left the Chair, the thanks of this Meeting was unanimously voted to the Chairman for his able and impartial conduct in the Chair.

At the close of the Meeting it was resolved to have a Public Dinner of the Inhabitants of the Town and Neighbourhood, on the Town Hall.

Tickets, 5s.—Dinner and a Pint of Wine included.

father's most famous poem 'The Village', written only a few years before this jolly encounter took place:

On the third day we reached Parham and I was introduced to a set of manners and customs, of which there remains, perhaps, no counterpart in the present day. My great-uncle's establishment was that of the first-rate yeomen of the period. . . . His house was large, and the surrounding moat, the rookery, the ancient dovecot and the well-stored fishponds, were such as might have suited a gentleman's seat of some consequence; but one side of the house immediately overlooked a farmyard, full of all sorts of domestic animals, and the scene of constant bustle and noise. On entering the house, there was nothing at first sight to remind one of the farm: a spacious hall, paved with black and white marble, at one extremity a very handsome drawing-room, and at the other a fine old staircase of black oak, polished till it was as slippery as ice, and having a chime-clock and a barrel-organ on its landing places. But this drawing-room, a corresponding dining parlour, and a handsome sleeping apartment up stairs, were all tabooed ground, and made use of on great and solemn occasions only – such as rent-days, and an occasional visit with which Mr Tovell was honoured by a neighbouring peer. At all other times the family and their visitors lived entirely in the old-fashioned kitchen along with the servants . . .

On ordinary days, when the dinner was over, the fire replenished, the kitchen sanded and lightly swept over in waves, mistress and maids, taking off their shoes, retired to their chambers for a nap of one hour to the minute. The dogs and cats commenced their siesta by the fire. Mr Tovell dozed in his chair and no noise was heard. . . . After the hour had expired, the active part of the family were on the alert, the bottles (Mr Tovell's tea equipage) placed on the table; and as if by instinct some old acquaintance would glide in for the evening's carousal, and then another, and another. If four or five arrived, the punchbowl was taken down, and emptied, and filled again. But, whoever came, it was comparatively a dull evening, unless two especial Knights Companions were of the party. One was a jolly old farmer, with much of the person and humour of Falstaff, a face as rosy as brandy

Shire Hall, Woodbridge

Ipswich

could make it, and an eye teeming with subdued merriment; for he had that prime quality of a joker, superficial gravity: the other was a relative of the family, a wealthy yeoman, middle-aged, thin and muscular. He was a bachelor and famed for his indiscriminate attachment to all who bore the name of woman – young or aged, clean or dirty, a lady or a gipsy, it mattered not to him; all were equally admired. He had peopled the village green; and it was remarked that, whoever was the mother, the children might be recognized in an instant to belong to him. Such was the strength of his constitution, that, though he seldom went to bed sober, he retained a clear eye and stentorian voice to his eightieth year, and coursed when he was ninety . . . so soon as his voice began to be elevated, one or two of the inmates, my father and mother for example, withdrew with Mrs Tovell . . . but I, not being supposed capable of understanding much of what might be said, was allowed to linger on the skirts of the festive circle . . .

Crabbe the Younger grew up to become the vicar of Bredfield in Suffolk. Powerful in build, genial in manner, slovenly in dress, he was so generous to the poor that his daughters were said to take the prudent precaution of rifling his coat pockets every time he left the house. The warmth of his personality won him the nickname of 'the Radiator' from his parishioner and friend, Edward Fitzgerald, translator of that unique and exquisite work The Rubaiyat of Omar Khayyam.

Fitzgerald had actually been born in Bredfield. Educated at Bury St Edmunds and at Cambridge, he became a friend of Thackeray and Tennyson but, spurning the London literary scene, chose to return to his birthplace and pursue the life of a leisured gentleman of letters, composing verses, translating the dramas of Calderon from Spanish, and living in a modest thatched cottage in the company of a retriever, a cat and a parrot named Beauty Bob. A passage from one of his polished letters leaves one in little doubt about the wisdom of his choice:

I read in the morning the same old books over and over again, having no command of new ones: walk with my great black dog of an afternoon, and at evening sit with open windows, up to which china roses climb, with my pipe, while blackbirds and thrushes begin to rustle bedwards in the garden, and the nightingale to have the neighbourhood to herself.

Of Fitzgerald's sheer delight in his native county there can be no doubt. He once referred to Ipswich as 'the Florence of Suffolk' and, writing to his father-in-law, the Quaker poet Bernard Barton, he skilfully justified the landscape which Cobbett found so uninspiring: 'A line of distant hills is all we want in Suffolk. A landscape should have that image of futurity in it.'

In 1860 Fitzgerald moved to Woodbridge where, in 1876, after an interval of nearly twenty years, he was visited by Tennyson, now Poet Laureate. Fitzgerald, himself a vegetarian, lived simply but, according to that other literary giant, Thomas Carlyle, this 'lonely, shy, kind-hearted man . . . discharged the sacred rites (of hospitality) with a kind of Irish zeal'. Fearing his own residence insufficiently grand Fitzgerald arranged for Tennyson to stay in The Bull on Market Hill. A few days after Tennyson's departure Fitzgerald congratulated old John Grout, the landlord, on having had such a distinguished guest under his roof. Grout remained singularly unimpressed: 'Dessay, anyhow, he didn't fare to know much about hosses when I showed him over my stables!'

In June 1883 Fitzgerald wrote to a friend:

If I do not write, it is because I have absolutely nothing to tell you that you have not known for the last twenty years. Here I live still, reading, and being read to part of my time; walking abroad three or four times a day, or night . . . pottering about my garden and snipping off dead Roses . . . and now and then a visit to the neighbouring Seaside, and a splash to Sea in one of the Boats. I never see a new Picture, nor hear a note of Music, except when I

drum out some old Tune on an Organ. . . . So I go on living a life far too comfortable as compared with that of better and wiser men: but ever expecting a reverse in health such as my seventy-five years are subject to . . .

Two days later he was dead.

A decade after Fitzgerald's death a small iron plate was fixed near his grave to record an entirely fitting tribute to his memory:

This Rose Tree Raised in Kew
Gardens from Seed Brought by
William Simpson Artist-Traveller
from the Grave of Omar Khayyam
at Naishapur was Planted by a few
Admirers of Edward Fitzgerald
in the name of the Omar Khayyam
Club. 7th October 1893.

Although Charles Dickens was par excellence *the chronicler of London and chose to live for preference in Kent, he knew East Anglia well and used it as a setting in his writings.*

The ancient Maypole inn which figures so prominently in Barnaby Rudge *is, in fact, The King's Head at Chigwell. Eatanswill, where Pickwick experiences old-style electoral corruption at first hand was modelled on the Suffolk market town of Sudbury. (The gross venality of the 1841 contest led to the town's disfranchisement by special Act of Parliament in 1844, so Dickens' satire is scarcely exaggerated.) The Angel in Bury St Edmunds makes much of its Dickens' connection to this day and Yarmouth, undisguised, plays an important role in the life of David Copperfield.*

It cannot, however, be claimed that Dickens' admiration was unqualified. As a young man in his early twenties he wrote testily to a friend that: 'If any one were to ask me what in my opinion was the dullest and most stupid spot on the face of the Earth, I should decidedly say Chelmsford.' Yet only a couple of

Ploughing

Flood at a brewery

years later we find the novelist describing a harvest scene on the road between Sudbury and Bury St Edmunds in language that is positively lyrical, almost loving. Mr Pickwick and Sam Weller are whirling along on a stage-coach in the last days of its glory, just before the railway intrudes itself upon a timeless scene:

There is no month in the whole year in which nature wears a more beautiful appearance than in the month of August. . . . Orchards and corn-fields ring with the hum of labour; trees bend beneath the thick clusters of rich fruit which bow their branches to the ground; and the

Somerleyton Hall, near Lowestoft

Wreck of the 'Cromer Express' at Witham in 1905

corn, piled in graceful sheaves, or waving in every light breath that sweeps above it, as if it wooed the sickle, tinges the landscape with a golden hue. A mellow softness appears to hang over the whole earth; the influence of the season seems to extend itself to the very waggon, whose slow motion across the well-reaped field, is perceptible only to the eye, but strikes with no harsh sound upon the ear.

As the coach rolls swiftly past the fields and orchards which skirt the road, groups of women and children, piling the fruit in sieves, or gathering the scattered ears of corn, pause for an instant from their labour, and shading the sun-burnt face with a still browner hand, gaze upon the passengers with curious eyes. . . . The reaper stops in his work, and stands with folded arms, looking at the vehicle as it whirls past; . . . You cast a look behind you, as you turn a corner of the road. The women and children have resumed their labour: the reaper once more stoops to his work: the cart-horses have moved on: and all are again in motion.

Dickens' affection for the region remained undimmed. Near the close of his life he wrote to his friend and biographer John Forster with urgent enthusiasm:

Chigwell, my dear fellow, is the greatest place in the world. Name your day for going. Such a delicious old inn opposite the churchyard – and such a lovely ride – such beautiful forest scenery – such an out-of-the-way rural place – such a sexton! I say again, name your day.

It has been cruelly observed that East Anglia is in effect an island, cut off on three sides by water and on the fourth by British Rail. Sardonic humour at the expense of the region's railway system has a long history. The novelist Thackeray observed as though making a profound philosophical statement:

'Even a journey on the Eastern Counties must have an end at last.' The Times of Saturday 17 October 1846 really let rip on the subject:

We do not really know what to do with this unnatural corporation. They are hard at it again. From Shoreditch to Yarmouth their whole line is a scene of . . . wild merriment and frantic adventure. . . . Cambridge trains go to Hertford and Hertford trains go off and are never heard of again. We do predict with the utmost confidence that there will in a few years be a veritable county tradition of some lost Parliamentary train plying about Ely and Brandon, like the *Flying Dutchman* round the Cape, with phantom stokers and ghostly passengers. . . . Our paper last week conveyed almost daily notifications of catastrophes or delays, and on Thursday we were obliged to condense into a pregnant paragraph the multitudinous mishaps that had occurred since the last announcement. Happily, no great damage has fallen on life or limb, but the worst results to the social and moral condition of the people are impending . . .

East Anglia is demoralized. A sentiment analagous to that most fatal effect of servitude which makes the slave hug his fetters is rapidly developing itself throughout this devoted district. Men declare they like travelling on the railway. They snatch a fearful joy from the romantic and hazardous character of the expedition, and would regard it as a spiritless and unstimulating incident if they were taken to the right station, with entire limbs, and in proper time. That yearning of Byron's hero for –

. . . all that gave
Promise of pleasure, peril of a grave,

is transferred to the hitherto sober and secluded peasant of the fens . . . and is roaring and ramping over the sandy warrens of Norfolk. This will never do. . . .

A windmill near Great Yarmouth

Binham Priory

On the move

An entirely unexpected benefit of railway building was the stimulus it inadvertently gave to archaeology. William Wire, a Colchester watchmaker, was a keen student of Roman antiquities:

17 June 1842

Purchased of a railway laborer, who found it near the viaduct, Lexden, a silver gilt hand-in-hand mediaeval ring with following legend engraved on it, JESUS NAZARENE.

26 August

Mrs Alston of London showed me a first brass coin of Hadrian, very much corroded, said to have been found in the rampart near Lexden Lodge, when cut through for the Eastern Counties Railway in July last.

30 August

The 'navvies' continue digging but find nothing.

29 September

Mr Cuthcent gave me an iron cannon ball found in the field adjoining the railway station, which was probably shot from the town during the Siege.

20 November

Went to the railway on Tuesday last, when I was informed that the day before that a fluted Roman urn had been discovered in a field south of the Station.

9 January 1843

Mr Gilbert informs me that he and the Revd H. Jenkins of Stanway had been trying to discover what Roman roads diverged from this town and that they had in a great measure been successful, one of which he said passed through the centre arch of the railway viaduct, Lexden.

It was not, however, all gain:

11 May 1843

When I was walking up Balkon Hill, I saw that a portion on the North side of the Balkon Fort had been destroyed in order to build additional rooms to the King's Head Inn to command a view of the railway. What a pity that one of the best preserved remains of Roman times should be destroyed to administer to the sensual pleasures, as it may be considered only as a decoy to induce persons to enter the house to drink.

The third Reform Act of 1884 gave the vote for the first time to the agricultural labourer and it was in East Anglia that labourers seized the initiative in sending one of their own number to Westminster. But he was not a local man. Joseph Arch was Warwickshire born; but his success in organizing Britain's first agricultural union in the 1870s made him a national figure. The men of Norfolk welcomed him as one of their own:

In the November of 1885 came the general election and with it my chance of entering Parliament. I was told that the working-men of North-West Norfolk had been holding meetings at their branches and had determined to have me as their candidate. They asked me to contest the seat and promised, if I would stand, that my expenses should be paid. They sent for me to go down to the Blackfriars Hall at Lynn when the candidates were selected. There were two liberal candidates for the vacancy; Sir Bampton Gurdon, whom the well-to-do and upper classes wanted to return, and myself, whom the labourers wanted to represent them. I went down, and when the poll was taken I polled exactly double the number of votes Sir

Newmarket

Bampton did. I therefore stood in the Liberal and labour-ing class interest. My opponent was Lord Henry Bentinck. . . . Lord Henry Bentinck was a young man and of course trained in a very different school; with the best will in the world he could not possibly enter into our feelings and understand our particular needs. The two millions of new voters wanted someone of their own class to speak for them. I was ready. The voting took place at Lynn on Tuesday 8th December 1885 and the votes were cast up on the Wednesday, when it was found that I was returned by a majority of 640. . . .

There was a great scene when the poll was declared. I remember how put about the Tories were, for a Liberal had not captured the seat for sixty or seventy years. They sent a troop of men down to one of my meetings to cripple me. They gave them five shillings and a gallon of beer each; but it so happened that a new line was being cut to South Lynn, and all the navvies knew me – the majority had come off the land on to the line.

One day the ganger went to Lynn to draw the money to pay the men, and on his way he called in at a public house, and overheard the men who had been sent down by the Tories discussing the best way to pay me out. That night he told the navvies what he had heard, and they all attended my meeting armed with sticks. When the Tory crowd commenced to set about me, the navvies went for them and thrashed them most unmercifully and the Tory roughs, with the navvies' marks on them, were regularly cowed and slunk out of the way.

I remember I rode through Lynn to the Town Hall in a donkey cart; and after the poll had been declared . . . I said that while my opponents with carriages, horses, servants, and all their aristocratic paraphernalia had failed to accomplish their object, Joseph and his brethren had accomplished their object with a donkey cart. The humble donkey had drawn me on to triumph and a majority of 640.

The day I entered Parliament as Joseph Arch MP for North-West Norfolk was a proud one but pride was subdued by responsibility . . . if I was smiling, it was an inside smile at the thought that my entry marked the triumph of our enfranchisement. I took my place in the Council Chamber of the nation as the representative of the labourer and the Prince of Wales – the Sandringham estates are in the North-West Division – and I said to myself 'Joseph Arch, MP, you see to it that neither the Prince nor the labourer has cause to be ashamed of you.'

Ask at random what sort of hunting one would associate with East Anglia and the answer might well be, through association

with the Fens or marshy coastlands, wild-fowling. But the novelist Anthony Trollope, with humorous self-deprecation, makes it clear that riding to hounds had a strong following in Essex:

Essex was the chief scene of my sport. . . . Few have investigated more closely than I have done the depth, and breadth, and water-holding capacities of an Essex ditch. It

The Avenue, Sandringham

will, I think, be accorded to me by Essex men generally that I have ridden hard. The cause of my delight in the amusement I have never been able to analyse to my own satisfaction. . . . I am too blind to see hounds turning, and cannot therefore tell whether the fox has gone this way or that. Indeed, all the notice I take of hounds is not to ride over them. My eyes are so constituted that I can never see the nature of a fence. I either follow someone, or ride at it with the full conviction that I may be going into a horse-pond or a gravel-pit. I have jumped into both one and the other.

If Trollope was comparing himself with the redoubtable Sir Claude de Crespigny he had cause for modesty, a quality little known to Sir Claude:

Where is Reynard making for? He must be an old marsh fox. Shall we catch him? On we go, only three or four of us left, right on the marsh land . . . and to the salt water, the tide being at its full height. . . . Where is he? He must have taken to the open water; some few of us wait there for a few minutes. The bay is studded with small islands. . . . About three hundred yards away we see something moving. . . . Our blood is up, and the excitement intense. Up comes a gentleman in a green coat and hunting cap. 'Here, take this,' he says, throwing down his hunting cap and coat, and with a cheer to the hounds to follow, he leaps head first into the water, followed by two and a half couple of hounds. It is our worthy baronet, Sir Claude de Crespigny. . . .

With breathless anxiety we looked on, fearing the cold and cramp might affect the bold baronet. . . . Presently he gained the island and a scuffle took place between the hounds and the fox and all went into the water. The hounds got back onto the island, but no fox. But it was not all over, for, to our amazement, we saw the baronet diving, and to our joy and wonder he came up, holding the fox aloft. Was there ever before such a hunting scene? Or will there ever be such again? . . . with the heartiest congratulations to Sir Claude on his wonderful feat of endurance, pluck and courage, we went home, full of joy and delight at having seen something we had never seen before and would never see again.

Sir Claude's icy plunge (the event took place in February) evidently did him no harm. Thirty years later, in an autobiography entitled, Forty Years of a Sportsman's Life *(1910) he set down his personal credo:*

A good many people . . . have chosen to set me down either as a man quite reckless of life and limb, or as an advertiser on a big scale. . . . As a matter of fact, I cannot lay claim to either distinction, having never actually courted danger for its own sweet sake, and never risked my life and limb for the petty purpose of self-advertisement. However, there is a whole difference between risking your life through sheer ignorance of its value, and shunning danger when by so doing you must soil the escutcheon of bravery, which should be the most precious possession of every good Englishman. . . . For myself, I must go further, and declare it is necessary, unless we are to perish like the Romans in the lap of peace and luxury, that some of us should strive to keep alive the reputation which Englishmen have always had of greatly daring and suffering all things. Surely when there is a daring deed to be done in any part of the world, an Englishman should leap to the front to accomplish it.

If some hunted from motives of patriotism others found a substantial, if indirect, professional benefit arising from the activity, as an obituary of the painter Robert Nightingale of Maldon reveals:

... his natural love of horses took him often into the hunting-field, where he followed the hounds with much enthusiasm, and these proclivities bringing him into familiar intercourse with people of a better class were of great use in advancing him in his profession. He not only painted his patrons' horses but also their favourite hounds, and occasionally their fat cattle. His fame as an animal painter became well-known and he had commissions to paint some hundreds of horses during his long working life, and notably painted some of the best animals in England for some of the greatest sportsmen of the day. There is no doubt but that his skill in this particular branch became so great as to excel even that of the great Landseer ...

Norfolk is classic shooting country. In 1861 the then youthful Prince of Wales purchased Sandringham for the very purpose of indulging that passion. A tenant farmer on the Sandringham estate has left an account of a day's royal pleasure which, while understandably jaundiced by the damage and disruption which attended it, nevertheless conveys a grudging admiration for the spectacle:

A complete silence having been secured for miles round, the day was ushered in by a procession of boys with blue and pink flags, like a Sunday School treat, a band of gamekeepers in green and gold ... an army of beaters in smocks and hats bound with Royal red, a caravan for the reception of the game, and a tailing off of loafers to see the fun, for HRH is very good-natured in allowing people to look on at his amusements, provided they do not interfere with them, and, if it could be conveniently managed, would perhaps have no objection to everybody's life being 'skittles and beer' like his own.

At about 11 o'clock the Royal party ... range themselves in a long line under the fences or behind the shelters put up for that purpose ... The boys and

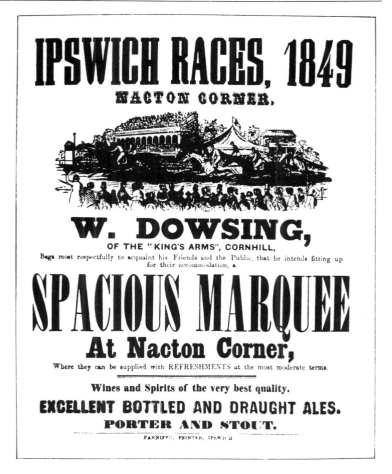

beaters are stationed in a semi-circle some distance off, and it is their place to beat up the birds and drive them to the fences, the waving flags frightening them from flying back. On they come in ever increasing numbers, until they burst in a cloud over the fence where the guns are concealed. This is the exciting moment, a terrific fusilade ensues, birds dropping down in all directions, wheeling about in confusion between the flags and the guns. ...

Gamekeepers?

Unwillingly at school?

A wild open country was the proper place for these military manoeuvres instead of highly cultivated farms; for on the partridge-driving days, if the Royal party did not do any individual harm, the village boys made it a Carnival, enjoyed trampling down all before them, breaking fences and gates, and doing as much mischief as they could . . .

Historians have conventionally taken the passage of Forster's Education Act in 1870 as marking the effective introduction of mass education in Britain. But it was another quarter of a century before schooling was both free and compulsory. In rural areas like East Anglia the enforcement of attendance proved a constant battle. The withdrawal of child labour (whose contribution Dickens had so casually noted in his description of a Suffolk harvest scene) threatened to disrupt not only the rural economy but the social order as well, for, as one of Her Majesty's Inspectors noted despairingly in 1877: '. . . the farmer will not let his daughter – nor his son except in earliest years – sit beside the children of his labourers'. The log books of the 'Board School' at Ashdon in north Essex reveal a twenty year struggle against the rival attractions of rural life:

The shooters then retire to another line of fencing, making themselves comfortable with campstools and cigars until the birds are driven up as before, and so on through the day . . .

It requires good, steady marksmanship for this style of shooting (for involving neither danger nor fatigue it can hardly be called 'sport') and the birds have one chance of escape; indeed . . . the old ones become quite strategical and know the flags are their friends and fly back through them, or veer round to the right or left out of range. This is altogether superior to the pheasant battue, when the birds are brought up in hen-coops and turned out tame into the woods to be shot down in thousands. . . . The hares are dispatched upon a still lower scale of slaughter, and they might as well have fired into a flock of sheep in a fold, an amusement which I am thankful to say did not suggest itself to them, or I tremble to think of what the uncompensated consequence might have been.

15–20 June 1879

Several Camps children away all week Carlick (leek) picking.

6–10 October 1879

Very thin school: harvest not finished.

26–30 July 1880

A bad week. Flower show in Ashdon on Tuesday. Sunday School Treat at Walden on Wednesday: school closed. Thursday very poor school. Children too tired to attend.

20–24 December 1880

Very poor school this week. Tuesday – nearly all the children away seeking Xmas gifts.

23 December 1881

Very thin school on Wednesday. Children away 'boxing'.

15 January 1884

3 children left school this week in consequence of the Uncle being summoned by the Board for employing the boy.

4 October 1889

Attendance bad again during the week. Gleaning not yet finished. . . . The Inspection being just after harvest is a great drawback, it being almost impossible to make up lost ground.

4 November 1892

Many of the children away gathering acorns. Unless a better attendance is enforced it is useless to expect good enough results to obtain the Higher Grant.

17 August 1894

Harvest work has been going on a fortnight. Several of the older boys are away leading horses.

24 July 1895

30 children absent gathering Wild Flowers for Ashdon and Bartlow Show tomorrow.

30 October 1896

The attendance is very irregular. Children are called

upon to assist in various kinds of outdoor work as acorn-gathering, potato-picking, root-pulling and sheep-minding.

9 August 1897

63 children absent. Of these only 5 are harvesting. For the remainder there would appear to be no adequate excuse.

Awaiting a royal visit, Norwich, 1909

Tennis, Edwardian Essex

21 January 1898

A meet of the hounds at Walton took away a number of children this morning.

10 February 1898

40 absent. 13 are suffering from colds. . . . The remaining 27 are merely 'wanted' to help at home.

Other regular causes of absence were ill-health and severe weather:

21–25 July 1879

Monday and Tuesday exceedingly wet: many children absent whole week in consequence.

17–21 November 1879

Heavy fall of snow of Friday kept many children away.

22 September 1882

Reopened school this week with a very small number. 13 only present out of 77 owing to gleaning and an epidemic of measles and scarlatina.

Other epidemics are recorded in 1891 (influenza, scarlet fever and mumps), 1892 (whooping cough), 1895 (diphtheria, whooping cough and measles) 1903 (whooping cough) 1907 (measles) 1908 (fever). In 1909 there was an outbreak of ringworm: 'I think I shall be justified in excluding all boys who have this complaint, even if they wear skull caps.'
Once a decent quorum had been assembled there then remained the problem of actually teaching them:

4 January 1886

Punished E. Cooper with three strokes (sharp) on the behind for pushing a boy off the form.

14 January 1886

Punished Ben Marsh with four strokes for inking the desk.

24 February 1886

Punished whole of Standard III for repeated idleness by three strokes on the hand.

13 April

Had to severely punish A. Nutting for disobedience and unruly conduct . . .

20 May 1886

Punished A. Nutting and sent him home as he showed signs of determined resistance . . .

Despite a parental thrashing as well A. Nutting was back in the book again in June and August:

10 August 1886

I am inclined to think that the boy is regularly stupid. Punished him but does not appear to have much effect.

If A. Nutting registered prominently through sheer persistence one of his class-mates achieved the dubious distinction of a uniquely original offence:

9 December 1886

Punished W. Ford for offering stolen glue to the other boys as Toffy and also for insolence.

One of C.E. Benham's Essex Ballads *(1895), entitled 'These New-fangled Ways', while satirizing rustic philistinism does so with a certain tongue-in-cheek sympathy:*

*Despite such discouragement the author of a school textbook – *
Essex Past and Present *(1900) – a Fellow of the Royal*
Geographical Society, no less, expressed the pious and rather
patronizing hope of better things to come:

. . . even now many of the people living in the country
districts of Essex do not go far from their own parish; and
in some remote parts of the county a farm labourer will
say that he is 'going foreign' when he is only going into a
neighbouring parish, two or three miles away. It is also
firmly believed that a letter to the nearest market town
could not be delivered if the word 'Essex' were not added
to the address. As education advances, so the country
people will gradually, but surely, gain a desire to see more
of their own country, and thus lose these old-fashioned
ideas.

Me, nao, sir, I don't howd 'ith these Board Schools.
Thay larn the booys too much, my thinkin', now.
An' what I see, there's jest as many fools,
As when thay put the young uns to the plough.

I howd 'ith larnin, mind, but let 'em larn
Saime way as I did, not that stuff o' theirs;
Larn 'em the proper way to thetch a barn,
Larn 'em the way to sao a field o' tares.

Geoggerfy! Now what on arth's the sense
A larnin' of 'em how the Moon go roun'?
An' all about Ameriky and France,
An' plaices tother side o' Lunnon town?

Education and emigration, railways and newspapers were
gradually eroding the isolation of East Anglia as the new
century opened. But, as the village war memorials still silently
bear witness, it was the holocaust of 1914–18 which swept
away for ever that Old England which had seemed so survive
so little touched so near the nation's greatest city. The memorial
at Bunwell, Norfolk, provides a fitting epitaph for a vanished
age:

Ye that live on in England's pastures green
Remember us and think what might have been.

1914

Bibliography

Sabine Baring-Gould; *Mehalah: A Story of the Salt Marshes*, 1880.

Letitia Beauchamp-Proctor; *Journals*, 1772.

C.E. Benham; *Essex Ballads*, 1895.

George F. Bosworth (ed.); *Essex: Past and Present*, 1900.

A.F.J. Brown; *Essex People 1750–1900*, 1972.

Sir Claude Champion De Crespigny; *Forty Years of a Sportsman's Life*, 1910.

William Cobbett; *Rural Rides*, 1830.

George Crabbe; *The Borough*, 1810

George Crabbe the Younger; *The Life of George Crabbe*, 1834.

Mrs Gerard Cresswell; *Eighteen Years on the Sandringham Estate*, 1887.

Daniel Defoe; *A Tour Through the Whole Island of Great Britain*, 1724–6.

W.A. Dutt; *Some Literary Associations of East Anglia*, 1907.

Wm. Dugdale; *The History of Imbanking and Draining*, 1772.

John Evelyn; *Diary* (ed. E.S. de Beer), 1959.

Edward Fitzgerald; *Letters and Literary Remains* (ed. W.A. Wright, 1889.

Robert Gibson; *Annals of Ashdon*, 1988.

Alfred Hedge; *Inns and Inn Signs of Norfolk and Suffolk*, 1976.

T.M. Hope; *An Essex Pie*, 1951.

Stan Jarvis; *Essex Pride*, 1984.

Miles Jebb; *East Anglia: An Anthology*, 1990.

Wm. Kempe; *Nine Daies Wonder*, 1600.

C.R. Leslie; *Memoirs of the Life of John Constable*, 184

John Ray; *The Wisdom of God manifested in the Works of Creation*, 1691.

Robert Reyce; *Breviary of Suffolk*, 1618.

Charlotte Fell Smith; *An Anthology of Essex*, 1911.

Gerald Solomons; *Stories behind the Plaques of Norwich*, 1981.

E.S. Symes; *The Story of the East Country*, n.d..

R.J. Thompson (ed.); *King Cole's Essex*, 1949.

Anthony Trollope; *Autobiography*, 1883.

Thomas Tusser; *Five Hundred Points of Good Husbandry*, 1571.

H.G. Wells; *Mr Britling Sees it Through*, 1916.

W.H. Weston; *A School History of Essex*, 1909.

Acknowledgements

I should like to thank Dolphyn Prints of Coggeshall for their assistance. The credits and information on all illustrations used in this book are given in page ascending sequence. The source refers to the photographer or the possessor of the illustration (RT = Richard Tames; PF = Paul Felix; BB = Barry Beattie).

Page **2** Harvesting, *RT*; **3** The Market Place, Norwich, *RT*; **6** Smacks, Lowestoft, *RT*; **7** Essex from the Thames, *RT*; **8** Saffron Walden, *PF*; **9** River Orwell, *PF*; **11** Gorleston Parade, *RT*; **16** Kentwell Hall, Long Melford, *RT*; **17** East Dereham, *PF*; **18** Theberton House, *RT*; **19** East Dereham, *RT*; **20** Clacton-on-Sea, *Tendring District Council*; **22** Cathedral gardens, Chelmsford, *PF*; **23** Keep of Hedingham Castle, *RT*; **24** Mound of Plashet Castle, *RT*; **26** Norwich Cathedral, *PF*; **27** Templar church at Little Maplestead, *RT*; **28** Map of Essex, *RT*; **29** Map of Essex, *RT*; **30** Kemp's nine days wonder, *RT*; **31** Fields of rape, mid-Suffolk, *B. O'Farrell, Mid-Suffolk Tourist Information Centre;* **32** Hengrave Hall, *RT*; **35** Lavenham, *BB*; **36** Orford Castle, *RT*; **37** Framlingham Castle, *RT*; **38** Cavendish, *PF*; **39** River Brett, *Brabergh District Council;* **41** Duel, woodcut of 1590, *PF*; **42** Fields of Lavender, *RT*; **43** Stokesby, Norfolk Broads, *PF*; **44** Brass of a Lord, *RT*; **45** Brass of a Lady, *RT*; **46** Portrait of William Harvey, Essex physician, *RT*; **48** Hedingham Castle, *Hedingham Castle;* **49** Aythorpe Roding, *BB*; **50** Lees Priory, *RT*; **51** Somerleyton Hall, *RT*; **52** A Summer's afternoon on the river, Norfolk, *RT*; **53** The Dunmow Flitch, *RT*; **54** River Gipping, Ipswich, *RT*; **55** Gun Hill, Southwold, *RT*; **56** Southwold, *RT*; **57** All Saints Church, Dunwich, *RT*; **58** Pulls' Ferry, Norwich, *RT*; **60** Lavenham, *BB*; **61** Sheringham, *PF*; **62** Norwich Cathedral, *RT*; **63** Portrait of John Ray, naturalist, *RT*; **64** Beeston Priory, *PF*; **65** Steeple Bumpstead, *BB*; **67** Book plate, *RT*; **68** Norwich, *PF*; **69** Thurne, Norfolk, *PF*; **71** Coggeshall, *RT*; **72** Siege of Colchester, *RT*; **73** Coggeshall Abbey, *RT*; **74** Dick Turpin, *RT*; **75** An Essex Butcher, *RT*; **76** Maze, Saffron Walden, *C.G. Hale;* **77** River Blackwater, *RT*; **79** Lowestoft beach, *RT*; **80** Wanstead House, *RT*; **81** Portrait of Daniel Defoe, *RT*; **82** Empire Day, Coggeshall, *RT*; **83** Bow bridge, *RT*; **84** Church End, Great Dunmow, *BB*; **85** St Osyth, *RT*; **87** Paddling, *RT*; **88** St John's Abbey gate, Colchester, *PF*; **89** Colchester, *RT*; **90** Chelmsford in the mid-eighteenth century, *RT*; **91** Cattle market, Norwich, *RT*; **92** Ipswich, *PF*; **93** Harwich, *RT*; **94** Market Hill, Sudbury, *RT*; **96** Middleton Tower, *RT*; **97** Nave of Norwich Cathedral, *RT*; **98** A Yarmouth 'Row', *RT*; **99** Cromer, *RT*; **100** Nelson's Monument, Yarmouth, *RT*; **101** Audley End, *RT*; **102** Newmarket, *RT*; **103** Oulton Broad, *RT*; **104** Leigh-on-Sea, *RT*; **105** Castle Acre Monastery, *RT*; **106** Holkham Hall, *RT*; **107** Cromer, *RT*; **110** Preparing Asparagus, *RT*; **111** Baptismal font in Walsingham church, *RT*; **112** Dedham, *RT*; **114** Colchester Castle, *c.* 1830, *RT*; **115** The College, Farmlingham, *RT*; **116** Alderton church, *RT*; **117** Flatford Mill, *PF*; **118** Crabbe's birthplace in Aldeburgh, *RT*; **119** Storm, Aldeburgh, *RT*; **120** Wendens Ambo, *BB*; **121** Bildeston, *BB*; **122** Abbey, Bury St Edmund's, *RT*; **124** The watersplash, Kersey, *Brabergh District Council;* **125** March for democracy, *RT*; **126** Shire Hall, Woodbridge, *RT*; **127** Ipswich, *RT*; **129** Spoof theatre poster on an unpopular government, *RT*; **130** Paddling, *RT*; **131** Flood at a brewery, *RT*; **132** 'The Maypole' in *Barnaby Rudge* as sketched by 'Boz',

RT; **133** Somerleyton Hall, Near Lowestoft, *Somerleyton Hall*; **134** Wreck of the 'Cromer Express' at Witham in 1905, *RT*; **136** A windmill near Great Yarmouth, *PF*; **137** Binham Priory, *RT*; **138** On the move, *RT*; **140** Newmarket, *PF*; **141** The railway comes to Colchester, *RT*; **142** Race notice, *RT*; **146** Game-keepers?, *RT*; **147** Unwillingly at school?, *RT*; **148** Kett's Castle, Norwich, *RT*; **149** Old Swan Inn, Saffron Walden, *RT*; **150** Awaiting a royal visit, Norwich, 1909, *RT*; **151** Tennis, Edwardian Essex, *RT*; **152** Thaxted, *RT*; **154** Waltham Abbey, *RT*; **155** 1914, *RT*.

Index

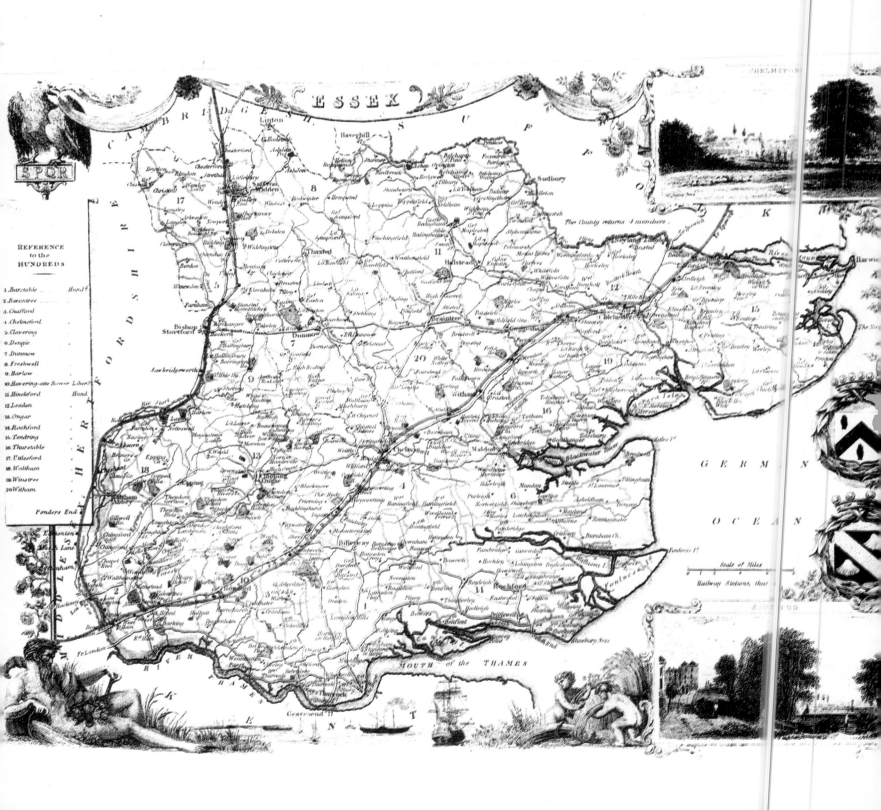

ESSEX

REFERENCE
to the
HUNDREDS

1. Barstable   Hund^d
2. Becontree
3. Chafford
4. Chelmsford
5. Clavering
6. Dengie
7. Dunmow
8. Freshwell
9. Harlow
10. Havering-atte Bower Liber.
11. Hinckford   Hund.
12. Lexden
13. Ongar
14. Rochford
15. Tendring
16. Thurstable
17. Uttlesford
18. Waltham
19. Winstree
20. Witham

The County returns 4 members.

CAMBRIDGESH.

SUFFOLK

HERTFORDSHIRE

MIDDLESEX

GERMAN OCEAN

RIVER THAMES

MOUTH of the THAMES

Gravesend R^r

Scale of Miles

Railway Stations, thus